Collective Behavior

Collective Behavior

ELEMENTS OF SOCIOLOGY
A Series of Introductions

Collective Behavior

Richard A. Berk
Northwestern University

WM. C. BROWN COMPANY PUBLISHERS
Dubuque, Iowa

SOCIOLOGY SERIES

Consulting Editors

Ann Lennarson Greer
University of Wisconsin-Milwaukee

Scott Greer
Northwestern University

Contents

In Memory Of Earny Trent,
Johnson Lochlear, Merle Chavis,
and Bobby Squires

Preface

I undertook writing an introduction to collective behavior with considerable ambivalence. Too often, elementary textbooks in sociology are misleading because even despite the best intentions, authors are severely constrained by a variety of factors beyond their control. First, the body of knowledge which sociology can currently provide is rather meager. Lacking compelling theory, overviews of most substantative areas are organized through conceptual typologies implying more rigor than actually exists. And even when a plausible theoretical framework is presented, findings are frequently equivocal. In the few cases when theory and data form a useful package, the practical implications are typically trivial. Students are justified in their reaction of "so what?". Second, introductory textbooks must gloss over many subtle and important issues. Faced with the necessity of summarizing, authors can either present a half truth as if it were the whole truth, or resort to cop out qualifiers. ("All other things being equal," finding A "suggests" conclusion B.) Both solutions do students an injustice by either providing misleading information or rendering the material practically useless.

Third, frequently elementary textbooks (and research in general) present the subject matter as if it rested on pure objectivity. Obviously, such is not the case. All knowledge must be evaluated within the context of an historical period and the biases of its scholars. Unfortunately, blinders are most difficult to remove even when social science insight is consciously turned inwards upon the authors and their culture.

Despite these fundamental problems in presenting sociological knowledge, introductory courses will obviously continue, and overviews of sociology will be employed. Faced with this prospect, and with the nagging sense that I should put up or shut up, I decided to try my hand at textbook writing. Hopefully this attempt reflects an effort to minimize some of the more salient difficulties with textbooks.

In dealing with the limitations of sociological knowledge, I have tried to emphasize not just what I believe to be true, but what I believe to be false. Scientific knowledge advances most directly from the elimination of false hypotheses about the world, not from the affirmation of those which are true. In the field of collective behavior, many earlier views have been refuted, and this is no small accomplishment. Yet the reader who expects to find all the answers herein will be severely disappointed.

Summarizing complicated issues is more difficult to handle. Where possible I have tried to include sufficient complexity to communicate the necessary subtleties. More important, considerable effort is directed toward presenting the strengths and weaknesses of various perspectives on collective behavior. Hence, this book is a critical examination of the field from which readers should develop their own analytical skills. None of my conclusions should be accepted simply because they possess the apparent legitimacy of appearing in print. Be skeptical.

Most difficult is the issue of biases which are a product of my own blinders and the blinders of twentieth century American culture. Where possible I have tried to be introspective and deal with issues as fairly as I can. However, since some distortion will inevitably appear, it is useful to state their sources out front. First, I believe that large amounts of human activity can be understood through the application of scientific methodologies. I do not deny that valid insights can be gained from art and literature, but I see these forms as complements of, and not replacements for, social science. Second, I am committed to making social science useful. Acquiring knowledge can be an enjoyable end in itself. However, I doubt that our society can afford ivory tower social scientists who avoid dirtying their hands with practical problems. At the risk of sounding overly theatrical and a bit egotistical, "If you're not part of the solution, you're part of the problem." Third, I am very much a product of the "New Left" activities of the 60's. Ideology is not a dirty word for me, though I try to retain a healthy amount of skepticism. Despite the fact that my foresight is far less that 20-20, ideology can imply vision. Probably more important, the past ten years have made me profoundly cynical about anyone who holds power. Power seems to magnify human frailty.

One final point. I have tried to write a book that will be challenging, yet not overwhelming to students in their first sociology course. No statistics of any kind are needed, sociological jargon is minimized, and important points are illustrated with examples. To those students for whom I have missed the mark, I wish to direct an apology in advance. There is no reason why a textbook should not be interesting.

Many people have assisted me while this book was being written. The sociology department at Northwestern University has lived up to its reputation for congenial and stimulating colleagues. I could always find good advice, sound criticism, and tennis partners as obsessed with competition as I am. Equally important were my teaching experiences with Northwestern undergraduates. I have now taught several courses in collective behavior and have learned from students every time.

A large number of people were also instrumental in actual preparation of the manuscript. Sarah Fenstermaker Berk took time from tennis matches and her own sociological pursuits to insightfully comment (sometimes a bit too candidly) on initial drafts. Pam Richards was most helpful in editing the manuscript and indicating where I was making very little sense. Finally, Fran Cohen, Mary Belda and Lynn Troyanowski managed to squeeze in long hours of typing despite their other duties.

1 | An Introduction

SOCIOLOGISTS seem to have a knack for inventing complicated words to describe rather common things. Sometimes these labels are necessary to minimize confusion, at other times they are a source of confusion themselves. Unfortunately, the label "collective behavior" falls into this second camp. There is wide disagreement among sociologists about the nature of "collective behavior", and considerable debate about whether a distinct type of human activity exists which should be singled out for this special name. Hence, the term "collective behavior" can include a great variety of actions, and ultimately may become so muddled as to have no useful meaning.

In this book we shall examine some of the more influential views on "collective behavior". Many of the perspectives discussed will be in conflict with one another, and any given analysis of "collective behavior" may tell more about the political views of the commentator than the empirical events described. For example, some theorists writing at the turn of the century were European aristocrats whose social position was threatened by the growing political power of new industrial classes. Since this politicization of the masses was frequently expressed through disruptive crowds, aristocratic per-

ceptions of "collective behavior" typically reflected a "conservative" bias. Conversely, many socialist writers during this same period had a "leftist" bias. In short, actions defined as "collective behavior" often have important implications for the stability of society and the safety of its citizens. Therefore, analyses of "collective behavior" are unusually subjective.

What is "collective behavior"? Probably the best way to be introduced to the phenomenon is through several examples. The first example is taken from an incident which occurred in the Spring of 1972 at a large Midwestern University. Students had gathered at a University plaza to hear speeches about a recent escalation in the Vietnam War, the mining of Haiphong Harbor. During the meeting the student body president proposed a referendum on a campus strike. Many sought far more militant action (like a take-over of local Republican election headquarters), others preferred a long term strategy of electing peace candidates. Nevertheless, the vast majority were angry at the escalation and frustrated with their inability to affect national policy on Southeast Asia. We pick up the action as students were leaving the meeting to return to their dormitories. They had been en-

1

couraged to spread news about the referendum and generate the widest possible participation in the vote scheduled for that evening.

To go from the plaza to the dormitories, many had to travel north. The most direct route led to Sheridan Road, a large city thoroughfare running the length of the campus. Rather than use the sidewalk, about half chose to take the middle of the street. This act was unnecessary and clearly defiant. Though the traffic was light, the students were a potential inconvenience to drivers.

During the strike of 1970, Sheridan Road had been a center of activity. Blockades were erected which seriously disrupted rush hour traffic; and students remembered the blockades as the strike's most effective and exciting activities. Earlier that day, when talk of a student strike first appeared, some students discussed blocking Sheridan Road. They noted its symbolic value in relation to Nixon's blockade of Haiphong Harbor.

From where students spilled out onto Sheridan Road to about three hundred yards north, were about 250 "jaywalkers." They walked in groups of five or six and their talk reflected diverse motives. The student clusters could not accurately be characterized as a march, since there was no organization, no interlocking of arms, no parallel lines of marchers, and no slogans, banners, or chants. Small groups were simply strolling down the middle of a main street about twenty feet apart.

The "jaywalking" continued about five minutes until one student ran to a wooden fence (near some construction), and tried to break off a section to move onto the street. He called to two friends for help, and together they dragged enough fencing across the road to block it completely. They yelled to students behind them and ahead of them to return and erect a barricade. Sheridan Road became the new arena and attention focused on the activity around the fence.

About two hundred students (the majority) responded; the rest continued north. People were still in clusters of three to ten with those closest to the fence the most aware of what was happening. Groups of people converged rapid-

ly to within a half block but only about thirty actually approached the fence. Most remained on the sidewalks and grass areas on either side of the road.

At first, many opposed the barricade. They said it would "turn people off," that nothing would be gained and that it misrepresented popular sentiment. Those in favor argued they were "bringing the war home," that there was no time for democratic decision-making, and that disruption was needed to arouse anti-war sentiment. At this point, the students who felt most keenly about the issues, seemed to be around the fence. Their movements were animated, their voices loud, their speech rapid. The less intense students stood on sidewalks and nearby grass areas talking calmly. By the fence arguments developed and many clear and cogent points were made.

The next three minutes were especially critical for the evolving crowd behavior. Three students had "siezed the time" when they began to construct a barricade. It seemed clear to everyone that the three probably could not finish the job alone. (At the very least the crowd would have to remain passive.) Hence, the act of tearing the fence and dragging it across the road was primarily a symbolic call for action and students at the barricade responded by beginning many simultaneous "negotiations." Various proposals were made and debated: "This barricade stuff is stupid and risky because it is destruction of property. Why don't we just stage a sit-down here in the street instead?" "What you guys are doing is too risky. You'll be arrested or suspended. I know it's just not worth that much to me. Why don't we just go along with the strike?" "A barricade will just turn people off. I don't want any part of it. I'm going back to the dormitory." Observers on the sidewalks engaged in similar discussions, in a lower key. Much talk seemed almost academic, as if what they did would have no consequences.

This talk led to various decisions. Some finding the barricade alien to their values and suspecting that moderation was impossible, simply left. Some argued for more "constructive" activities, but departed when it became clear that many intended militant action. Among those in sympathy with the barricade who remained, many disagreed about the degree of disruptiveness that should be encouraged. Some favored a temporary human barricade, while others suggested that Sheridan Road be "liberated" until the Haiphong blockade was lifted. A few preferred "trashing" of downtown stores. Nevertheless, the idea of a barricade soon gathered enough support that increasing numbers of people moved from the sidewalks to the road, while others began to collect more building materials.

Within minutes it was clear that those wanting to erect a barricade would do so, while those opposed would not intervene. With about about fifty people following in the street and fifty more supporting the fence, the barricade was moved a block and a half south to a main intersection. More material was added: parts of another fence, boards from a nearby construction site, and large trash receptacles. In ten minutes a substantial structure was built and about 250 students were milling around, many still arguing. An active minority strongly endorsed the barricade. A smaller though equally active minority opposed it. Most students seemed undecided but eventually chose temporarily to support the barricade, or least to let it stand.

Despite many differences of opinion there were no longer two distinct crowds. The physical boundaries which had earlier separated the apathetic from the concerned, now gave way. Some spectators could be observed at the barricade, while some activists were on the sidewalks. In short, the crowd was permeable and location in the gathering was no longer a good indicator of role.

Later, when students were asked what they had been thinking at this critical time, their answers differed. Even those most committed to the barricade (including persons later arrested trying to maintain it) were weighing many considerations. Should they make a "public anti-war statement", "bring the war home", generate a 1970-style strike, stimulate the militancy of 1970, embarrass the University President, and/or "train" political activists? Should they risk "turning off" the public, punishment from police or the University? Some felt cynically that no action would work and others wanted only to relax in the sun. Then too, many considered how friends and parents would re-

act to visible participation. Some were concerned by their desire to be leaders, and for others the actions meant a break from their lifestyle. The militants differed primarily in their tallying of costs and benefits. Though ambivalent, they saw the barricade as useful. Others believed it cost too much. Many could not decide.

In the hours that followed, the divisions of opinion did not change. The street was blocked and used as a forum for many speakers. Police were called, but did not move against the students or their barricade. Traffic was rerouted. Students remained into the night and fires were built for warmth. People brought guitars and small groups gathered in friendly fashion. The police stood by, and interacted cordially with students. There was no name-calling from either camp. Some students knew a few of the police, and it was made clear that the actions were not anti-police.

By 1:00 a.m., seventy-four students remained. By 4:00 a.m., thirty remained. At 5:15 a.m., the police told the remaining twenty-five that the barricade would be torn down at 5:30, and they could disperse or be arrested. Seven chose to stay. Morning rush hour traffic moved normally down Sheridan Road.

How might one characterize the building of the barricade on Sheridan Road? First, there was no evidence that the barricade was planned in advance. The decision to build the barricade and the manner in which it was to be constructed were produced at the scene. Second, the people involved were able to interact face-to-face. There was extensive communication among participants about the issues involved. Third, in order to build and hold the barricade, many crowd members had to be involved. A small group of students would have been unable to quickly block Sheridan Road and in fact, extensive cooperation

1. Richard A. Berk, "A Gaming Approach To Crowd Behavior," American Sociological Review, June 1974.

among the students greatly facilitated the effort. In summary, one might describe the events as spontaneous, concerted group activity, generated through face-to-face interaction.

Traditional approaches to crowds have focused on events like those described above. In this volume a somewhat broader view will be taken. "Collective behavior" is far more common than is usually suggested, involving groups of people under many different circumstances. Our second example is a description of incidents from the My Lai massacre. The reader should look for parallels to the events on Sheridan Road.

As Brooks' second platoon cautiously approached the hamlet, a few Vietnamese began running across a field several hundred meters on the left. They may have been Viet Cong, or they may have been civilians fleeing the artillery shelling or the bombardment from the helicopter gunships. Vernado Simpson, Jr., of Jackson, Mississippi, saw a man he identified as a Viet Cong soldier running with what seemed to be a weapon. A woman and a small child were running with him. Simpson fired. . .again and again. He killed the woman and the baby. The man got away. Reporter Roberts saw a squad of GIs jump off a helicopter and begin firing at a group of people running on a nearby road. One was a woman with her children. Then he saw them "shoot two guys who popped up from a rice field. They looked like military-age men . . .when certain guys pop up from rice fields, you shoot them." This was the young reporter's most dangerous assignment. He had never been in combat before. "You're scared to death out there. We just wanted to go home."

The first two platoons of Charlie Company, still unfired upon, entered the hamlet. Behind them, still in the rice paddy, were the third platoon and Captain Medina's command post. Calley and some of his men walked into the plaza area in the southern part of the hamlet. None of the people were running away; they knew that U.S. soldiers would assume that anyone running was a Viet Cong and would shoot to kill. There was no immediate sense of panic.

The time was about 8 A.M. Grzesik and his fire team were a few meters north of Calley; they couldn't see each other because of the dense vegetation. Grzesik and his men began their usual job of pulling people from their homes, interrogating them, and searching for Viet Cong. The villagers were gathered up, and Grzesik sent Meadlo, who was in his unit, to take them to Calley for further questioning. Grzesik didn't see Meadlo again for more than an hour.

Some of Calley's men thought it was breakfast time as they walked in; a few families were gathered in front of their homes cooking rice over a small fire. Without a direct order, the first platoon also began rounding up the villagers. There still was no sniper fire, no sign of a large enemy unit. Sledge remembered thinking that if "there were VC around, they had plenty of time to leave before we came in. We didn't tiptoe in there."

The killings began without warning. Harry Stanley told the C.I.D. that one young member of Calley's platoon took a civilian into custody and then "pushed the man up to where we were standing and then stabbed the man in the back with his bayonet. . . The man fell to the ground and was gasping for breath." The GI then "killed him with another bayonet thrust or by shooting him with a rifle. . . .There was so many people killed that day it is hard for me to recall exactly how some of the people died." The youth next "turned to where some soldiers were holding another forty or fifty-year-old man in custody." He "picked this man up and threw him down a well. Then [he] pulled the pin from a M26 grenade and threw it in after the man." Moments later Stanley saw "some old women and some little children—fifteen or twenty of them—in a group around a temple where incense was burning. They were kneeling and crying and praying, and various soldiers. . .walked by and executed these women and children by shooting them in the head with their rifles. The soldiers killed all fifteen or twenty of them. . ."

There were few physical protests from the people; about eighty of them were taken quietly from their homes and herded together in the plaza area. A few hollered out, "No VC. No VC." But that was hardly unexpected. Calley left Meadlo, Boyce and a few others with the responsibility of guarding the group. "You know what I want you to do with them," he told Meadlo. Ten minutes later—about 8:15 A.M.—he returned and asked, "Haven't you got rid of them yet? I want them dead." Radioman Sledge, who was trailing Calley, heard the officer tell Meadlo to "waste them." Meadlo followed orders: "We stood about ten to fifteen feet away from them and then he [Calley] started shooting them. Then he told me to start shooting them. I started to shoot them. So we went ahead and killed them. I used more than a whole clip—used four or five clips." There are seventeen M16 bullets in each clip. Boyce slipped away, to the northern side of the hamlet, glad he hadn't been asked to shoot. Women were huddled against their children vainly trying to save them. Some continued to chant, "No VC." Others simply said "No. No. No."

By this time, there was shooting everywhere. Dennis I. Conti, a GI from Providence, Rhode Island, later explained to C.I.D. investigators what he thought had happened: "We were all psyched up, and as a result, when we got there the shooting started, almost as a chain reaction. The majority of us had expected to meet VC combat troops, but this did not turn out to be so. First we saw a few men running. . .and the next thing I knew we were shooting at everything. Everybody was just firing. After they got in the village, I guess you could say that the men were out of control."

Brooks and his men in the second platoon to the north had begun to systematically ransack the hamlet and slaughter the people, kill the livestock, and destroy the crops. Men poured rifle and machine-gun fire into huts without knowing—or seemingly caring—who was inside.

Roy Wood, one of Calley's men who was working next to Brooks' platoon, stormed into a hut, saw an elderly man hiding inside along with his wife and two young daughters: "I hit him with my rifle and pushed him out." A GI from Brook's platoon, standing by with an M79 grenade launcher, asked to borrow his gun. Wood refused, and the soldier asked another platoon mate. He got the weapon, said. "Don't let none of them live," and shot the Vietnamese in the head. "These mothers are crazy," Wood remembered thinking. "Stand right in front of us and blow a man's brains out." Later he vomited when he saw more of the dead residents of My Lai 4.[2]

The tragedy of My Lai involved a variety of complex factors. We cannot take the time here to discuss most of the relevant issues. However, from the point of view of "collective behavior" one can note many of the same phenomena that were apparent on Sheridan Road. Much of the activity was spontaneous, concerted, and generated by groups of people in close contact with one another.

Most analysts of crowds would agree that our two examples reflect considerable "collective behavior". As a final example, we turn to a series of actions in the United States Congress. At first, this example may seem very different from the others. Indeed, most traditional views would argue that "collective behavior" is not involved at all. Later a case will be made that the traditional views are misleading.

How the Democrats Bungled the Price Rollback

Washington—On March 28, Cost of Living Council Director John Dunlop spent an uncomfortable morning with House Banking Committee Republicans. They told him that Phase 3 was in deep political trouble, that Congress was itching to legislate tougher price controls, and that the administration seemed headed for a certain political defeat in the House.

Michigan's Garry Brown, one of the Congressmen present, remembers the admonitions. "We generally told him the administration's request for a simple extension of wage-price control authority was dead," he recalls.

Three weeks later, however, the simple extension of the Economic Stabilization Act requested by the administration sailed through the

2. Seymour M. Hersh, *My Lai 4,* (New York: Random House, 1970), pp. 48-52.

House unscathed. All Democratic efforts to impose price ceilings and rollbacks, and to otherwise toughen up the controls program were defeated overwhelmingly.

The most common explanation for this surprising turnabout is that the House caved in to the business lobbyists who swarmed over Capitol Hill. And lobbying certainly was a key factor. But even more important was the bungling of House Democrats. Without their political ineptitude, it's doubtful the administration could ever have won its victory.

Indeed, the Democratic defeat can serve as a case study of how intramural wrangling and weak leadership can sometimes turn certain victory into sharp defeat. Responsibility in this case must rest on the strife-ridden House Banking Committee, which managed to turn the legislation into a political liability, and House Speaker Carl Albert, who failed to lead effectively.

"Carl Albert was more concerned about getting votes for extending the west front of the Capitol than with the control bill," says one bitter House Democrat. "That's real priorities for you."

"We never dreamed the Democrats could pull us through by fouling up so badly," confesses one administration official.

Initially, the controls legislation seemed tailor-made for White House foes in Congress. Phase 3 plainly wasn't working and the public clamor for tougher controls was growing by the day. The legislation would be considered right in the middle of the highly visible consumer meat boycott, and at a time when wholesale prices registered their most shocking rise in over twenty-two years.

The Nixon administration's own lobbyists were bringing back ever more gloomy news to their downtown bosses. The Senate had passed a bill imposing some mandatory rent controls, and inflation was heating up even more as the House took up the measure. "Realistically, we had given up on our simple extension," recalls one administration lobbyist. "Most of us felt the House was going to do something horrendous that would make the Senate bill look great in comparison."

Even Wilbur Mills, probably the shrewdest analyst of congressional sentiment, flatly predicted the House would approve severe price rollbacks and a freeze. When the House Banking Committee held hearing last month, most of its Democrats agreed on a bill that would rollback prices and interest rates to March 16 levels, then impose those levels as ceilings. Almost half the committee's Republicans also were anxious to approve a tough bill.

The bill, as drawn up by committee Democrats, had its share of problems. First, the freeze was to be of indefinite duration, and could be lifted by the President, on a case-by-case basis, only when he found it was causing "gross inequities." Then too, as originally written, the measure seemed likely to cause political and economic difficulties by including raw agricultural products and even market interest rates in the rollback. Further, the legislation encroached on the jurisdiction of other congressional committees in setting up a vast consumer counsel office and moving to regulate credit for commodity futures trading.

Despite all this, the legislation was given a fair chance of making it through the House—until the committee actually started to write the bill in public session. Then, in an uproarious session, some committee members started competing to see who could sound and act the toughest in going after the "price gougers."

The clear winner was Chicago Democrat Frank Annunzio, who proposed rolling back all food prices to May 1, 1972 levels. With support from a few conservative Republicans, anxious to kill the bill, and urban Democrats, fearful of consumer protests, the panel approved this measure twenty-three to eleven. Nobody was more surprised than Mr. Annunzio. "I never would have offered it, if I thought it would carry," he later admitted.

At this point, the House Democratic leadership stepped in. Realizing that such a severe measure never could pass the floor, Mr. Albert and others worked feverishly overnight with some committee members to repair the damage. The next day the Democrats endorsed a proposal which "only" rolled back all prices and interest rates to levels prevailing Jan. 10, the last day of Phase 2. "In that emotional atmosphere, we really believed this was a moderate proposal," recalls one distressed Democrat.

This version got through the banking panel, but immediately ran into a roadblock at the more conservative Rules Committee, which must clear all legislation for House action. Typically, the Democratic response was to quickly improvise a patchwork substitute that rolled back most prices and non-market interest rates to March 16 levels. This cleared the Rules Committee, but by this time the whole situation was in shambles.

"You have to be very sensitive when you start to formulate important legislation like this," notes Rep. Thomas Ashley (D. Ohio), a senior members of the banking panel. "When things start to go wrong, there tends to be a snowball effect. By the time we got this bill to the floor the damage was irreparable."

One of these insensitivities was the absolute exclusion of Republicans all along the way, even though a number of moderate and liberal GOP lawmakers favored a tough controls bill. These Republicans played almost no role in the Banking Committee's deliberations, and only at the last minute were they informed of the substitute bill before the Rules Committee. "We were never given a chance to vote for a viable alternative to Phase 3," complains Rep. Margaret Heckler (R. Mass.).

As a result, in an almost unprecedented show of unanimity, all House Republicans teamed up with a number of disgusted Democrats to defeat the substitute in a procedural vote and pave the way for the simple extension the President sought.

While the banking committee clearly mishandled the legislation, the House Democratic leadership did little to straighten things out, Although Speaker Albert and his cohorts said all along that the controls measure was a "priority" item for Democrats, the leadership permitted the situation to steadily deteriorate.

When House leaders finally did step in to try and correct the foulups, they vacillated back and forth between different strategies, ignoring the substance of any legislation. "The leadership has always let the committees handle these things and they just can't break this cord," complained Rep. Thomas Rees (D., Calif.).

It may be argued that Congress simply can't legislate effectively in an area so complex as specific controls covering the whole economy. If so, the leadership shouldn't have encouraged such a bill in the first place. In any event, once the legislative process begins, and a committee proves itself unable to deal with the complexities involved, then the function of effective leadership should be to straighten matters out.

But that isn't the way it worked this time, which points out a much bigger problem. Earlier in this session, the House Democratic leadership received credit for pushing through important procedural changes, which were intended to promote a more effective and responsive House. But these leaders still lack any real program, even in such a gut Democratic area as economic controls.

As long as this is true, the White House will continue to win most of its battles with the Democratic Congress. With opponents like this it's tough to lose.[3]

What do the three examples have in common? First, there are three parallels about which most crowd theorists would agree.

1. The behavior involved many people in extensive face-to-face contact with one another.

2. Much (or even most) of the behavior was not planned in advance; it evolved at the scene.

3. The group activity was rather transitory. Although each incident had ramifications, the collective action itself was short lived.

4. The behavior involved considerable cooperation among participants. That is not to say that everyone concurred or behaved completely in concert. Rather, there was an important amount of interdependency. One legislator could not pass a bill, one soldier could not have massacred a village of Viet-

3. Albert R. Hunt, "How the Democrats Bungled the Price Rollback" *The Wall Street Journal,* April 23, 1973, Reprinted with permission c. 1973 Dow Jones and Company, Inc. All Rights Reserved.

namese, and one student could not have built and held the Sheridan Road barricade.

There are at least three other parallels about which crowd theorists might disagree.

1. Individuals were acting on motives which reflected an attempt to obtain the "best" outcome in light of the situation. The group and its environment provided an *opportunity* in which certain types of participation might bring rewards. For example, helping to build a barricade might permit some students to feel they were shortening the war, raising public awareness about American foreign policy, or becoming a campus "heavy".

2. In deciding to act, each individual had to consider the chances that his/her action would gain support from others on the scene. Put yourself in the shoes of the soldiers at My Lai. Would you begin to shoot civilians if you thought you would be the only one who would? (It is also important to ask whether or not you would have shot civilians if others *were* doing so.) Put yourself in the shoes of the students on Sheridan Road. Would you start to build a barricade if you thought you would be the only person involved? Or, if you were a legislator, would you make an impassioned speech if you thought no one would listen and respond?

3. The people involved in all three examples had a variety of motives whose mix varied from person to person. On Sheridan Road, some students were interested primarily in anti-war actions, others were against the American System in general, and some were hoping to cut class. In short, as individuals operated under a variety of motives, the crowds reflected a variety of motives.

In summary, when discussing "collective behavior", this book will be referring to the behavior of people in crowds. That activity is transitory, not well planned in advance, involves face-to-face contact among participants, and considerable cooperation. Most modern collective behavior theorists would accept this characterization, though some might prefer an extension to include people not in face-to-face contact with one another (to describe phenomena like fads epitomized in the Hula-Hoop craze). Later in the book a case will be made that crowd activity also involves rational, goal directed action, in which possible rewards and costs are considered along with the chances of support from others in the crowd. Further, since people's rewards and costs depend on other crowd members, considerable negotiation occurs and much of the behavior that evolves reflects a series of compromises among participants. Hence, one can consider the generation of crowd behavior to be a result of a large informal meeting where people decide on a course of action.

For Further Reading

Chapter 1 has attempted to give readers an intuitive feeling for issues in collective behavior. There are a wide variety of other written sources for such insight.

Hayden, Tom. *Rebellion in Newark*. New York: Random House, 1967.

A description of the Newark Civil Disorder of 1967.

Hersey, John. *The Algiers Motel Incident*. New York: Bantam Books, 1968.

Hersey presents a compelling description of one tragic incident during the Detroit Civil Disorder of 1967.

Rude, George. *The Crowd in History*. New York: John Wiley and Sons, 1964.

Americans are not the only people who take to the streets. Rioting has been a popular European pastime for hundreds of years.

2 | Methodological Issues in the Study of Collective Behavior

NO science can be completely objective. Theoretical definitions and their operationalizations rest on scientific convention, measurement always contains error, and propositions are at best refuted, never completely supported. It is beyond the mission of this book to discuss epistemolgy,[1] but the reader can get some feeling for these issues by remembering that scientific "truth" is always in flux, with new findings supplanting old and new theories in constant evolution. Scientific "fact" depends fundamentally on its historical period. Recall that it was less than ten years ago when the saying "he has as much of a chance as putting a man on the moon" implied certain failure.

Since some subjectivity exists in all scientific work, differences of opinion are common. Recent writings on the origin of the solar system, for example, reflect considerable disagreement. Research on collective behavior has created unusual amounts of controversy which can be attributed to at least three factors endemic to empirical work on crowds. First, crowds often have important physical impact on the orderliness of society. When central cities are being burned by rioters, theories of collective behavior generate more than detached interest, and objectivity is severely threat-

ened. Second, explanations of crowds often suggest extensive societal criticism. For example, if one views a given riot as a spontaneous outburst against injustice, criticism of the society is obviously involved. For people with a blind allegiance to their society, this implied criticism may generate more hostility than serious thought. Such attitudes make objectivity less than likely. Third, data on crowds is typically poor. For a variety of reasons crowds are hard to study, and most theories of collective behavior have been based on shoddy empirical materials. In short, much of the writing on crowds has been produced with suspect data by persons having a particular axe to grind. No wonder controversy exists.

In the following chapters, conflicting views of crowds will be discussed in some detail. Before immersing ourselves in the substantive issues, it will be important to gain a better understanding of how such differences of opinion could occur. Without

1. Epistemology is the science or theory of *the method* of knowing about things. It addresses the question, "how do you know what you know?" For example, how do you know that two plus two is four? Given certain fundamental assumptions called axioms this statement can be proven mathematically. The way things can be proven in mathematics, and the study of what a proof really demonstrates, are examples of issues in epistemology.

an appreciation of these methodological considerations, it will be hard to decide which substantive views are more plausible.

The remainder of this chapter will be organized around the three factors listed above which contribute to the intense controversy. For the next few pages we will engage in some sociology of sociology.

WHY CROWDS PHYSICALLY THREATEN PUBLIC ORDER

During the recent wave of Civil Disorders in American cities, President Johnson authorized a Presidential Commission (the Kerner Commission) to study the events and make recommendations. Many important political figures were involved in the commission's work, and hundreds of thousands of dollars were spent to produce a comprehensive report. The disruptions created by Civil Disorders were of national concern.

Shortly after the Kerner Commission had issued its report, a series of studies were produced by the National Commission on the Causes and Prevention of Violence. Though touching on many types of violence in America, several of the studies focused on collective disruption. One report (The Walker Report) which generated particular interest discussed the violence surrounding the 1968 Chicago Democratic Convention. Part of the blame for the events was placed on overzealous demonstrators. More importantly, severe criticism was directed at Chicago Police who were accused of rioting against peaceful citizens. Again, local collective disorders had generated national concern.

Another example is the overreaction of prominent members of President Nixon's administration to the threat of collective disturbances at the 1972 Republican Convention. It seems that many representatives/officials of the federal government and the President's White House staff initiated widespread spying operations in an attempt to keep tabs on citizens supected of holding "unacceptable" political opinions. The justification for these blatant invasions of privacy (clearly in violation of the Bill of Rights) had been "National Security". Apparently, the administration felt that rioting (and other kinds of collective expression) posed a severe threat to the well-being of the country.

There are many other examples of governmental concern about collective violence. Race riots in Chicago in 1919 and in Detroit in 1943, along with Civil Disorders during the sixties in Newark, Detroit, and Los Angeles (Watts), all produced local commissions to investigate the events. Obviously, violent crowds generate concerted attention.

There are several reasons why the physical consequences of collective violence cannot be ignored by governments. First, violent crowds frequently endanger citizens and destroy large amounts of property. During one of the most brutal riots in American history, the New York City draft riots during the Civil War, as many as 2,000 people may have been killed. Property damage was estimated in the millions. The disorders were begun by draft-age men angered at being conscripted to fight an unpopular war.[2]

2. The Civil War was very unpopular with many Northerners. Today we sometimes think that freeing the slaves turned the war into a common crusade. In fact, ending slavery was not Lincoln's primary motive for fighting the war, nor was it a salient motive for most Northerners. Lincoln was trying to "preserve the Union" and maintain the economic dominance of the more heavily industrialized North. Most Northerners did not really understand these issues and had to be "sold" on the necessity of taking up arms.

(Sound familiar?) Not only were they against fighting white Southerners to free black slaves, they were fearful that freed slaves would compete with them in an already tight job market. More recent American riots have been far less violent. The Civil Disorders of the 60's usually had less than fifteen fatalities per riot, though property damage was at least as extensive as that in New York.

A second reason why riots generate such concern is that they usually trigger the application of counterforce. Hundreds of police are brought to the scene; often federal troops are introduced. When such massive forces are employed, millions of dollars are diverted from usual police and military activity and injuries and fatalities result. Often the society becomes more polarized. These undesirable consequences can occur even if the means of control are as humane as possible. When, as too frequently happens, the application of massive force is inappropriate, careless, and/or vindictive, the problems are far more severe. For example, throughout all the urban riots of the 60's, no compelling case for the existence of snipers was ever made. Yet initial reports from most riots claimed that snipers were active. Hence, drastic and dangerous countermeasures were employed. Windows supposedly used by snipers became targets for barrages of gunfire from pistols, high power rifles, shotguns, and automatic weapons. Many innocent citizens were wounded, some were killed. In retrospect, the alledged sniping seems to have been a result of poorly trained police and National Guard units firing at one another in the night. It's a good thing they weren't better shots.

In summary, collective behavior can physically threaten the public order through the actions of both crowd participants and forces introduced to control participants. Even if a given disturbance is not severe, the potential for growth is enough to generate intense concern on the part of authorities. Further, peaceful crowds gathered at football games, dances, political rallies, and rock concerts have riot capabilities. Large numbers of people and the spontaneity of the potential outburst can combine with other factors to produce a situation which could quickly become violent. For our discussion, the important point is that citizens and public officials are most concerned with how violent crowds are generated and how they can be controlled. Theories of crowds thus have important implications for the manner in which collective disorders are handled. Differences in opinion about the nature of collective behavior are taken most seriously by the actors because of these implications. For example, a theory of crowds stating that participants respond only to massive force can have important influences on the exercise of crowd control. Theorists who do not hold this view will be especially vehement in their opposition since the use of the "wrong" theory can have important practical consequences.

WHY CROWDS CAN THREATEN THE LEGITIMACY OF GOVERMENTS

As the extensive work of riot commissions suggests, crowds can have important ideological consequences as well as physical consequences. First, when a large number of people in face-to-face contact are disorderly, break laws, and/or cause injury and damage, a community is faced with massive disobedience. The message is often very clear: a group of citizens is collectively challenging the public order. Often unintentionally, the spectre of anarchy is raised. Obviously, societies cannot tolerate extensive disorder (societies are supposed to encourage stability, or at least contain disorder within certain bounds), or they cease to function. For example, when an alledged rapist is lynched, citizens are saying (*de facto*) that the criminal justice system is illegitimate. By "taking the law into their own hands," they communicate subversion of "due process." Since all societies rest on notions of law, societal foundations are challenged when the legal system is ignored or implicitly attacked.

A second type of ideological challenge hinges on explanations of crowd activity. If extensive crowd behavior is attributed to malfunctions in a society, direct societal criticism is involved. An example is the "Taxations Populaires" which frequently occurred in 18th century France. When poor harvests of wheat made bread too expensive, large numbers of citizens gathered at local bakery shops and took bread at what they felt to be a fair price. Their aims were rather modest: to have enough food to sustain a meager standard of living. Yet, the fact that citizens introduced their own "price controls" suggested that government economic and agricultural polices were ineffective. The historian Rudé tells us that severe bread riots in 1775 nearly toppled the French government, and crippled new economic programs based on supply and demand (rather than custom). Enemies of the new economic programs seized on the riots as popular reactions against societal malfunctions, and as indicators that the new policies were ineffective. In contrast, supporters of the program tried to blame the riots on "outside agitators" and "criminals." Note that the latter interpretations of the "Taxations Populaires" would have diluted criticism of the government since the fault lay with troublemakers, not the economy.

In short, if crowd activity can be blamed on criminals and misguided political activists, criticism of the society is minimized. On the other hand, if rioting is said to reflect "real" grievances, the people and policies responsible for the grievances come under attack. Spiro Agnew, when Governor of Maryland, may have recognized this when he "explained" the 1968 Baltimore civil disorder as follows: "It is no mere coincidence that a national disciple of violence, Mr. Stokely Carmichael, was observed meeting with local Black-Power leaders and known criminals in Baltimore on April 3rd, three days before the Baltimore riot began."[3]

A third type of ideological challenge develops directly from the expressed motives of crowd participants. Some crowds consciously communicate a specific set of grievances and/or ideological positions that explicitly attack the status quo. In 1842, England experienced a series of collective disorders as a result of rising grain prices and factory layoffs. This was also a period when working people were agitating for the "People's Charter" which, if adopted by Parliament, would have provided for a variety of basic rights including "universal manhood" suffrage. Many of the rioters openly endorsed the Charter, and such support was a clear challenge to the way England was being governed. When the "Plug-Plot" riots (so named because "turned out" workers marched from town to town stopping work by pulling out the plugs of factory boilers) became associated with the Chartist movement, they directly confronted the current regime.

To summarize, it is clear that the physical actions of crowds can directly challenge the social order. In addition, the physical activi-

3. *U.S. News and World Report,* Vol. 64, No. 17, April 22, p. 28.

ty, its interpretations, and related rhetoric often *communicate* that large numbers of people are dissatisfied with the status quo. Massive disregard for law, actions which imply specific grievances, and direct ideological attacks often carry important messages. All are threatening comments about the society and are grounds for concern among public officials and the general population. Hence, it should come as no surprise that commentators on crowds frequently have axes to grind. Since crowds can have such immediate and important effects, it is very difficult for crowd theorists to control their biases. This is one of the most important methodological problems in the field of collective behavior. Social scientists, like other people, have a stake in their societies (or in changing them) and sometimes cannot step back and view collective behavior as objectively as one might like. Some recent crowd theorists have been writing about collective behavior with smoke rising over their cities, angry students "liberating" their campuses, and police clubbing and gassing innocent citizens. Though such an atmosphere can generate insights about crowds, it is also likely to stimulate emotions that can distort those insights.

WHY THE DATA ON CROWDS IS INADEQUATE

Crowd activity involves a series of factors including causes, events at the scene of action, and the consequences of that action. From the researcher's viewpoint, each occurrence in the series presents different kinds of methodological problems. Difficulties arise because too often social scientists gather data where the methodological problems are the least severe, rather than where there is the greatest need for information. A commonly told story in research methods courses will illustrate the point.

A man is walking down a street at night and notices a drunk down on his hands and knees directly under a street light.

Man: What are you doing?
Drunk: I am looking for a quarter I lost.
Man: Where did you lose it?
Drunk: About half a block down the street.
Man: Then why are you looking here?
Drunk: Because here's where the light is brightest.

Collective behavior theorists too often work where the methodological light is brightest, instead of where the important substantive questions lie. This can result in misleading characterizations of crowds.

More formally, it is often useful to think of collective behavior as involving three stages. First, there are a series of prior conditions which affect crowds. Second, there are group processes and environmental factors at the scene. Third, there are the consequences of the collective behavior. Each stage has certain characteristics which influence the types and quality of data that can be gathered.

At first glance, it might appear quite difficult to study events which occurred prior to a given instance of collective behavior. Since crowd activity seems unpredictable, how would one know when to gather data in the expectation that collective behavior was about to occur? Usually, one cannot. However, much useful material is routinely gathered for other purposes which can be applied to the study of crowd pre-conditions:

a) Census Data—Many countries routinely count their populations and gather a variety of indicators of the "quality of life" (*e.g.*, amount of sub-standard housing, family income, family size). If one suspected that extensive grievances lead to riots, one might use this data to see if during periods of, for instance, housing shortages, their is a greater incidence of collective disorders.

b) Economic Indicators—Many countries routinely measure economic conditions using such indicators as unemployment, amount of production, bank interest rates, and profit margins. These indicators often reflect malfunctions and/or inequalities in a society which can lead to collective behavior. For example, periods of unemployment are often periods of violent strikes.

c) Local Official Statistics—Most political units (villages, towns, cities, counties, states) keep a variety of statistics. For example, police record crime rates, schools record amounts of truancy, hospitals record the number of patients treated, and Chambers of Commerce record economic growth. Like other official statistics, these records can be used to measure pre-conditions of crowds. If one suspects that rioters are likely to be criminals, one might see if neighborhoods with higher arrest rates are more likely to have riots. However, one important complication should be noted. Arrest rates may reflect not only the amount of "crime", but also the policies and efficiency of local police. It is well known that when police deploy more men in a given area, arrest rates usually increase. Clearly, the rate of crime has not gone up; rather, the increase results from a greater concentration of police personnel. If one interprets arrest rates as a pure measure of amount of crime, one's conclusions are likely to be faulty. Similar problems must be addressed in the use of all "Official Statistics."

d) Social Science Data Gathered for Other Purposes—With the growth of social science, the number of empirical studies going on in any given period has become quite large. Often data gathered for one purpose, say, to measure the causes of divorce, can be used to study crowd pre-conditions. If one suspects that neighborhoods with unstable family life are riot prone, a study on divorce may have important implications for the incidence of collective behavior.

e) Qualitative Historical Materials—One of the most useful sources of data on the pre-conditions of collective behavior is written documents in which historical events are described. For example, if one were studying a campus takeover by militant students, the college newspaper might have important information about events leading to the disruption. Or one might examine the speeches of student leaders as indicators of student grievances.

f) Retrospective Accounts—After an instance of collective behavior one can talk to persons involved in the events (rioters, police, public officials, etc.) and ask them to explain why the disruption occurred. For example, one might interview people arrested during a riot and ask them why they participated. Or, one might interview a knowledgeable observer like the editor of a local newspaper, seeking information on the causes of the disruption. However, one must be very skeptical of such material, since "Monday Morning Quarterbacking" is easy to do and often biased. Further, people's memories frequently distort the facts, especially when they have a vested interest in the events. One might get very different stories of the causes of a campus takeover from the college president and the student body president.

In short, there are a variety of ways one might assess pre-conditions for collective behavior. There are always weaknesses in any body of data, but in this case the problems are not crippling.

Probably the richest and most accessible data on crowds involves the consequences of crowd action. Once collective behavior occurs, one can use all the kinds of data available on crowd pre-conditions, plus a variety of other material. If the disruption is severe, police departments, fire departments, insurance companies and other organizations affected by the disturbance will have details concerning the consequences of the events. Further, even if the events do not draw the attention of such agencies, crowds often leave tangible traces of their behavior. If a party at a fraternity house turns into a brawl, one can easily assess the amount of damage. Or, if students stage a sit-in, one can tell which university functions are disrupted. However, like any data these kinds of material have weaknesses which must be considered. In the case of a student sit-in, some disruption may result from the actions of campus police, not students.

In contrast to the rich data on crowd pre-conditions and consequences, data on *crowd process* during collective behavior is sparse and largely inadequate. To understand what occurs during collective behavior one must know such things as what the leaders did, whether the crowd members knew one another, how crowd members reacted to the introduction of police, and what people in the crowd were actually doing (*e.g.*, sitting, standing, running, cheering, chanting, marching, etc.). Obviously, if one wants to understand crowds, details on behavior in crowds are necessary. Unfortunately, for a variety of reasons this type of data is very difficult to obtain:

a) Events during crowd behavior usually occur rather quickly.

b) Many events occur at once.

c) Actions are often taking place over a relatively wide geographical area.

d) The occurrence of collective behavior is difficult to anticipate, so that investigators interested in the phenomena usually miss the activities.

e) Mob process (as compared to the results of mob process) leaves few traces, and frequently the best one can do is gather retrospective accounts.

f) Crowd participants are unlikely to take time out from what they are doing and cooperate with an investigator. And even if they did, the suspicion that a researcher might be a police officer or informant would mitigate against a sincere interaction.

g) Crowd participants or persons who happen to be present during collective violence frequently have very salient vested interests in the interpretations of the phenomena. Their accounts are thus especially vulnerable to conscious and unconscious distortions.

h) The high risk of personal injury persuades many researchers to study crowds from a distance.[4]

For these reasons and others, data on collective behavior reflects an important gap. There is lots of material on the pre-conditions of crowds and lots on consequences of crowd activity. In contrast, there is little on crowds themselves. This situation would be bad enough, but when coupled with the high motivation and likely bias of many theorists, the results are sometimes incredibly bizarre. Where shaky data should encourage prudence, one finds wild speculations labeled as theory. In short, because of the immediate and important impacts of crowds, researchers who lack good data feel compelled nevertheless to theorize.

4. Richard A. Berk, "The Controversy Surrounding Collective Behavior: Some Methodological Notes," in *Collective Violence*, ed. James F. Short, Jr. and Marvin Wolfgang, (Chicago: Aldine, 1972).

There are several especially common errors in collective behavior theory that should be addressed briefly now. First, the reader should try to separate description from explanation. Consider a pot of bubbling, steaming water sitting on the burner of a stove. A young child notices the bubbling pot of water and asks you what's going on. A sensible answer might be that the water is "boiling." Note that you have only *described* what is occurring, *not* explained it. An explanation would involve a discussion of the effect of heat on liquids and the transformation of liquids to gases. As obvious as this difference might seem, it is often overlooked in crowd theories. For example, there are many instances of police breaking ranks against orders and attacking demonstrators. An observer might characterize the behavior as "contagion." What could the word mean? "Contagion" is a medical term referring to the spread of disease, and necessarily implies the existence of micro-organisms which carry the illness. Obviously, crowd behavior is not spread by germs. When used to describe crowds, "contagion" is at best a descriptive metaphor and not an explanation. Hence, when reading a characterization of collective behavior, the reader must always be prepared to ask (1) Are the terms employed descriptive or explanatory? and (2) Are the terms metaphorical or meant to be taken literally? There is nothing wrong with the use of metaphor *per se*. Problems develop when metaphors are used as if they were analytical explanations of crowd behavior and/or when they introduce ideas that are not thoroughly explicated. We will soon see that many crowd theories "explain" the phenomena with terms like "group mind", "suggestibility", "contagion", and "herd instinct". These are at best metaphorical descriptions and should not be confused with theoretical explanations.

One of the reasons that collective behavior theorists have been able to get away with metaphorical characterization is the absence of data on what is actually occurring in crowds. Since we really know very little about people's behavior in crowds, it is easy to slip into metaphor. In addition, critics have little information with which to challenge the metaphors. This absence of high quality data on crowd process leads to a second common error in theories of collective behavior. Researchers often extrapolate unjustifiably from events prior to crowds and the consequences of crowd activity to crowd behavior itself. A little story should provide an intuitive grasp of the problem:

It's another war movie on the late show. Humphrey Bogart is leading a tattered group of soldiers across the desert in North Africa. They are returning from a dangerous mission behind enemy lines and have run out of food and water. The sun is brutally hot and it looks as if they can last but a few more hours. Bogart keeps his men moving with hoarse patriotic appeals, threats of court martial, and examples of his own courage. The youngest soldier cracks under the strain and begins to cry hysterically. Bogart pulls the soldier up by his torn lapels, and slaps his face. The young soldier regains his composure with a "Thanks, I needed that", and they proceed. Finally they reach the top of a large sand dune and below they see a small water hole. The tired band summons enough energy to run wildly towards the water hole, but Bogart senses potential danger and shoots his pistol in the air to gain his men's attention. The water may be poisonous! With the men anxiously waiting around the water hole, Bogart tries to decide if the water is safe. Fortunately, the youngest soldier was studying to be a research chemist before he gave up school to answer duty's call. He examines the water carefully and decides that it is not too alkaline to drink. At that point everyone jumps into the water hole. They drink, splash, and dance about. All military discipline breaks down as the men cheer, yell, and generally make fools of themselves. Eventually, they drink their fill, fill up their canteens, and push on. Military discipline is restored, and Bogart again assumes his tough command. (And of course they get back safely.)

From our perspective, the important point is that one might have a very different analysis of events depending on what was observed. If only the behavior *in the water hole* was seen, the behavior would have been characterized as irrational "mob psychology", an example of man reduced to his basic needs. Grown men, (soldiers yet!) behaving like children. However, if one observed only the behavior preceding the outburst, the events would be described in very different terms. One might stress the great self control, sense of duty and tight military discipline. Obviously, an accurate picture would have to include the entire series of activities which occurred.

Let's assume that a researcher wanted to analyze the behavior just described. Let's also assume that the researcher *only observed the behavior in the water hole.* What would be a sensible way to handle the data? Clearly, only actions at the water hole should be considered, and not events before or after. However, if the researcher felt compelled to analyze the *entire series of events,* he/she could extrapolate from what was observed in the water hole, or in this case simply generalize under the assumption that the water hole behavior was a good sample of what occurred before and after. Thus, *all* the behavior would be characterized in the same manner; as childish and irrational. Obviously, this would be an inaccurate assessment of the events.

Analyses of crowds often involve the kinds of errors just described. Having in-complete information, especially about riot process, researchers carelessly extrapolate from the data they have. For example, some investigators of civil disorder noted that many people arrested during riots had prior criminal records. From this they extrapolated backwards in time from a riot consequence to the riot process and assumed that riots were *caused* by the actions of criminals. (This would be like assuming that since the soldiers behaved emotionally and without discipline while in the waterhole, they must have been emotional and without discipline earlier.) What these studies of Civil Disorders failed to note was:

1. Consequences of rioting (*i.e.,* the kinds of people arrested) are at best indirect hints about what occurred during the riot.

2. People with criminal records were not the only riot participants.

3. A person with a criminal record is not necessarily more riot prone.

4. Many people with criminal records *did not* riot.

5. There may be factors associated with having a criminal record, such as being unemployed, which are more important in explaining riot participation. In technical terms, the variable "criminal record" has a "spurious" relationship to riot participation.

The general point is that much research on collective behavior occurs where the methodological light is brightest. Since there is relatively good data on pre-conditions of crowds and crowd consequences, theories tend to be based primarily on these kinds of material. Unfortunately, there is relatively poor data on what actually occurs in crowds and many theories illegitimately generalize to crowd process from the pre-conditions and consequences.

A third common error in studies of crowds involves what social scientists call the "Unit of Analysis." Some theories apply to societies as a whole. For example, one might postulate that countries with higher unemployment will have more violent strikes. Some theories apply to smaller units, like organizations or groups. For example, factories paying lower salaries might have higher rates of worker unrest (perhaps measured through "slow downs"). Some theories apply to individuals, as in the case where people who have less trust in their government are more likely to participate in riots. Errors develop when data and theory from one unit of analysis (society, group, individual) are used at another unit of analysis.

Let's say someone has a theory stating that societies with greater "social strain" are more likely to have riots. "Social strain" might be defined as contradiction between the ideals of the society and its performance. For example, a society might be based on the notion that everyone is equal in the eyes of the law, but in fact wealthy people are less likely to be convicted of crimes than poor people even if both are indicted for the same offenses. This would generate "social strain." Note that even if the theory is correct, it applies to the society as the unit of analysis, and is not necessarily an explanation of why and how individual people riot. "Social strain" describes a characteristic of the society as a whole and not what may be going on in people's consciousness. People don't have "social strain." People might perceive the "social strain" but then one would have to develop a theory of how this occurs, and it would involve a psychological process, not a societal process.

Let's say someone has a theory that when people feel their government has not treated them fairly, they will be more likely to riot; a theory at the individual unit of analysis. Even if the theory is correct, it tells nothing about the functioning of the society at large. It describes psychological processes.

The essential point is that a theory developed to explain phenomena at one unit of analysis is usually misleading if applied to another unit of analysis. Unfortunately, too many theories of collective behavior fall into this trap.

A fourth common error in theories of collective behavior is to assume that all crowd participants behave alike. Many theories state that crowd members are dominated by nearly identical beliefs about their situation, have the same goals, and act in the same ways.

This assumption of crowd homogeneity can be attributed to at least two methodological problems. First, one must separate statements about the average or typical crowd member from statements about all crowd members. It is reasonable to say that "on the average", crowd participants behave in certain ways. But to then transform a statement about a typical person to all persons is incorrect. For example, an "average" urban policeman in the United States is a white male, about thirty-five years of age, from a working class background. However, not all, or even a majority of policemen fit this description. An "average" crowd member in a campus demonstration may be white, male, twenty years old, and from a middle class background. But again, not all demonstrators fit that description. Some commentators of student disruptions have explained the events in terms of rebellion against white middle class values. That may have some validity (though probably not much) for some demonstrators, but will obviously not work very well for non-white demonstrators from non-middle class backgrounds. Theorists who fail to distinguish typical crowd members with all crowd members often generate misleading generalizations.

A second reason why crowd theorists often slip into unwarranted assumptions of homogeneity gets back to the question of data about crowds. If the data on crowd process is poor, and lacking in detail, it is easy to assume that people are behaving alike. With not enough information to uncover how different people are acting, one may assume that they are acting similarly.

Most people have had the experience of looking down on pedestrians from a tall building. From great height the people are often said to look like "ants." What is really meant is that the people all look very much alike: one cannot distinguish men from women, whites from blacks, children from adults and so on. Of course, the people are quite different from one another, but from twenty stories up, one cannot see enough detail to make distinctions. Data on crowds has much the same problem. Lacking detail on what happens in crowds, one can get the impression that everyone is alike. Recent research based on better data clearly refutes the idea that crowd participants are homogeneous in biographical background, thought, and activity.

SUMMARY AND CONCLUSIONS

This chapter tries to make several points about methodological problems in the field of collective behavior. First, while no science can

be completely objective, work in collective behavior has been unusually vulnerable to bias. Second, the frequent bias can be attributed to the coupling of inadequate data on crowd processes with intense motivation and vested interest among investigators. Third, the methodological problems have generated a variety of common problems for collective behavior theorists. Four of the most pervasive are (1) confusion between description and explanation, (2) extrapolation from events prior to crowds and after crowds to crowd process itself. (3) shifting inappropriately from one unit of analysis to another, and (4) assuming homogeneity among crowd members. Now that these issues have been raised, we can begin to examine some of the more well known theories of collective behavior.

For Further Reading

Many collective behavior authors mention methodological issues in passing, but there are no books primarily concerned with research problems in the field. General research methods texts can be helpful, but are usually too detailed for an introductory course and cover a variety of subjects whose relevance to this text is marginal. About all I can suggest is three articles:

Berk, Richard A. "The Controversy Surrounding Analyses of Collective Behavior: Some Methodological Notes," in *Collective Violence* ed. James F. Short, Jr. and Marvin E. Wolfgang. Chicago: Aldine, 1972.

Many of the points made in that article have been covered in this chapter.

Fisher, Charles D. "Observing a Crowd: The Structure and Description of Protest Demonstrations," in *Research on Deviance* ed. Jack D. Douglas. New York: Random House, 1972.

McPhail, Clark. "Civil Disorder Participation: A Critical Examination of Recent Research" in *American Sociological Review* 36 (Dec.) 1058-1073.

This article may be too difficult for an introductory course, but for those who can manage it, very useful.

3 | Outdated Views of Collective Behavior– Le Bon, Freud, and Blumer

WITH all there is to learn about people in crowds, why should one examine outdated theories of collective behavior? There are at least four reasons for allotting space to discredited theories in an introductory text. First, many of the older views of collective behavior are still held by lay people. Terms like "mob psychology," "contagion," and "herd instinct" can be found frequently in media analyses of crowds and are common in everyday language. Some readers of this book may find their initial ideas about crowds very much in tune with this perspective. Second, though most earlier work on collective behavior has proven to be inaccurate, it produced several insights which have withstood considerable scrutiny. Third, a great deal of recent research on collective behavior has been generated in response to these earlier views. It is difficult to understand today's issues without knowing something of their history. Finally, the older theories provide a good intellectual exercise in which the student reader has a chance to use his/her critical powers. One shouldn't believe everything one reads, and these traditional theories provide an opportunity to practice healthy skepticism.

THE CROWD AS A "GROUP MIND"— GUSTAVE LEBON

Gustave LeBon is the grandfather of collective behavior theory. He wrote at the turn of the century when Darwin was drawing attention to the role of heredity in behavior and Freud was exploring the human unconscious. A popular medical issue of the era was hypnotism (though it was thought to be a somewhat unscientific concern). LeBon was able to draw on all three of these sources to develop a theory of crowds. His eclectic approach is to be praised; however, his work is very much a product of its time.

LeBon was also greatly influenced by the political issues of his day. France was undergoing its industrial revolution; earlier feudal and rural traditions were on the wane and new social classes were struggling to gain control of the country. A middle class, whose economic power rested on the new factory system and expanding markets, was challenging the power of aristocratic classes. Urban workers, often recent migrants to cities in search of jobs, were agitating for better working conditions and a larger voice in how the country was to be governed. Also visible were a variety of working class political movements, (typically left of center) seeking to seize control of budding capitalism and transform it into a system run by the "proletariat." In short, this was a period of very rapid social change accompanied by considerable violence. France was still feeling the effects of its first mass-based revolution a hundred years earlier. Several decades of war and internal unrest had combined with a period not unlike McCarthyism in the United States and the bigotry of the Dreyfus Affair to exacerbate societal tensions.[1] Even more fundamentally, France was being shaken at its economic and political foundations.

LeBon's basic sympathies lay with older traditions and the aristocratic classes. Hence, for him the period was extremely threatening. This helps explain LeBon's biases and many of the inaccuracies in his theory. When he spoke of crowds as irrational, herdlike mobs, part of this description rested on prejudices about the common people of his time and their challenge to his "better" world. Two passages will provide a flavor of LeBon's views.

Today the claims of the masses are becoming more and more sharply defined, and amount to nothing less than a determination to utterly destroy society as it now exists, with a view to making it hark back to that primitive communism which was the normal condition of all human groups before the dawn of civilization. Limitations of the hours of labor, the nationalization of mines, railways, factories, and the soil, the equal distribution of all products, the elimination of all the upper classes for the benefit of the popular classes, etc., such are these claims.[2]

LeBon was speaking about urban working class people, whose demands seemed alien and subversive. He had similar criticism for the middle classes, and was obviously not enamoured with their widening participation in French political life. Crowds come into the picture because Le-

Bon felt that street mobs were a common way the masses made their wishes known, and because many new forms of official political life, specifically parliaments, juries, and popular elections, functioned much like street mobs. Letting "the people decide" would, in LeBon's view, ultimately lead to the destruction of civilization even if the decisions were made through democratic political forms. Turning specifically to the details of crowd action LeBon began,

It will be remarked that among the special characteristics of crowds there are several such as impulsiveness, irritability, incapacity to reason, the absence of judgement and of a critical spirit, the exaggeration of the sentiments, and others besides—which are almost always observed in beings belonging to inferior forms of evolution—in women, savages, and children, for instance.[3]

Though the above quotations illustrate LeBon's questionable objectivity some of his insights on crowds have merit, and a wide variety of his ideas are still part of "common knowledge." Unfortunately, it is quite difficult to summarize LeBon's work on crowds. In many places his most famous book, *The Crowd*, reads more like a political tract than social science. Further, he often seems more interested in description than analysis, and it is difficult to distinguish metaphor from literal meaning. Finally, the book is badly organized, containing redun-

1. The Dreyfus Affair was an attempt by some French officials to cover up government corruption by framing a Jewish military officer (Dreyfus) for treason. Dreyfus was allegedly at the center of a plot to give military secrets to foreign countries. The attempt to use Dreyfus as a scapegoat was linked to a extensive anti-semitic propoganda, and though he was eventually vindicated, Dreyfus' career was ruined.
2. Reprinted with permission of Macmillan Publishing Co. From *The Crowd* by Gustave LeBon, p. 16.
3. LeBon, *The Crowd*, pp. 35-36.

dant passages and irrelevant asides. The overall result is a loosely, but often passionately argued treatise, rich in style but very hard to outline neatly. Nevertheless, a summary follows.

LeBon set the stage for his theory of crowds (which, incidentally, is also a theory of mass society) by emphasizing two broad trends in French society near the turn of the century. First, the old ways of life were being destroyed by a combination of government corruption and pressure from newer social classes. As a result, traditions and institutions that had maintained order in times past, could no longer sustain a smoothly functioning society. Second, while the older society was disintegrating, a new form of order had yet to evolve. Capitalism was still too young to provide the customs and institutions around which a stable society could be built. Hence, the masses were freed from all social bonds, and the country was increasingly at the mercy of its uneducated, rootless, and irresponsible citizens. (It is worth mentioning in passing that quite similar assessments were made by some observers of the American 1960's. The society—free enterprise, the work ethic, the family, morality, etc.—were coming apart with ignorant poor people and spoiled students in the vanguard tearing down the "system.")

With the societal background established, LeBon discussed two additional factors necessary for the formation of crowds. First, there must be a leader. "He [the leader] constitutes the first element in the organization of heterogeneous crowds...A crowd is a servile flock that is incapable of ever doing without a master."[4] LeBon characterized leaders as nervous, excitable types, bordering on madness, and having little sense of self-preservation. Leaders appealed

to unconscious needs and through a variety of techniques "hypnotized" crowd members. Hypnotic obedience to the leader replaced a sense of individual responsibility in crowd participants. LeBon apparently meant "hypnotism" literally, though at that time the mechanisms behind this process were not understood. (They are still not well understood.) Today, it is useful to interpret "hypnotism" as a metaphor, and then examine the ways LeBon claimed leaders manipulate crowds.

1. Leaders often resorted to *flattery* as a means of gaining control of a crowd. The flattery made crowd members feel important, able to challenge the society, and supportive of the leader. One can think of this process as a kind of seduction of crowd participants.

2. *Rhetoric* was also crucial. By rhetoric, LeBon meant the use of words appealing to unconscious needs (or on a simpler level, emotions), not rational thought.

3. Along with extensive rhetoric, leaders used *symbols* to appeal to emotions. For example, rather than explaining why Dreyfus should be tried for treason in terms of his alleged offences, a leader would emphasize that Dreyfus was a Jew, and that French, Christian morality was at stake. A leader at a street rally might make such an appeal after the playing of the French National Anthem, with the French flag on one side and a large cross on the other.

4. Leaders could increase their influence if they appeared authoritative and *prestigious*. Crowd members would be more likely to follow persons who were supposed to be leaders in other contexts.

5. Arguments for crowd action would be more effective if presented in an *affirmative*

---

4. LeBon, *The Crowd*, p. 118.

style. This meant that a leader would not present both sides of a controversy, but only present the side he wanted the crowd to accept.

6. Affirmative arguments would be more effective if they were *repeated* many times. If a series of ideas were presented often enough in a variety of ways, people would come to adopt them.

The second factor LeBon mentioned as important for crowd formation was the presence of a precipitating event that either drew people to the scene or focused attention on a particular issue. Here his analysis is especially vague, and he argued largely through example. Apparently, effective leadership was often not sufficient to motivate crowds, and some kind of happening was a necessary catalyst to action. Unlike leadership, a precipitating event was not always necessary, but only an important influence.

The combination of undisciplined, anarchistic masses, an effective leader, and a precipitating event produced crowds. What are crowds like? LeBon employed one overarching concept as a characterization of collective behavior. He spoke of the "Law of Mental Unity of Crowds": a law which apparently involved three related processes which produced a "Group Mind." First, "leveling" occurred in which individuals with a variety of characteristics were transformed into virtually identical beings. Regardless of age, sex, nationality, educational level, occupation, etc., once a crowd materialized, all participants felt, thought, and behaved in similar ways. Second, a crowd ceased to be an aggregate of individuals and became a single entity, almost like a new organism. One could speak of a crowd as if it were a structure unto itself. Finally, crowd behavior was "emergent." Crowds could not be understood as the summing of individual tendencies but only as a newly created being with unique characteristics and processes.

Metaphorically, one can compare LeBon's "Mental Unity of Crowds" with the creation of a biological organism from millions of cells. Just as one cannot understand the courting behavior of a moose from knowledge of its cellular structure, one cannot understand crowds from knowledge of the individuals who become participants. One must move to a large unit of analysis; from individual cells to the entire moose and from individual participants to the crowd as a whole. However, the analogy breaks down in one important aspect. Moose cells do different kinds of things and are combined into organs with specialized functions. LeBon would argue that such division of labor does not occur in crowds. For all practical purposes, with the exception of the leader, all participants are identical.

Given the "Law of Mental Unity" what were the consequences for crowd participants? What happened to them as a result of this process?

First, unconscious mental processes become salient. LeBon described these processes as akin to reflexes, emanating from the spinal cord, not the brain. Actions were no longer mediated by rational thought. Just as you would quickly lift your hand off a hot stove without thinking, a crowd member would riot without thinking.

Second, crowd members were extremely "suggestible." This meant in part, that participants would believe almost anything they were told, especially if the leader was effective and the hypnotic control complete. In addition, "suggestability" meant that crowd members were extremely vulnerable to suggestion from each other. A kind of chain reaction imitation process could occur in which people copied the actions of others. If one person started to run, all would be likely to follow. Also, emotions (as distinct from actions) could be transmitted from person to person. If one individual became angry, others were also likely to get angry. If one individual became frightened, so would others. Hence, emotional states could spread through crowds like a "disease," with "contagion" the mechanism. At times, LeBon spoke of "contagion" as an example of "hypnotic" effects of crowd members on each other.

Third, the kinds of thinking exercised by crowd members were very different from the kinds of thinking in other circumstances. "Normal" thought was characterized as linear and logical. A person's mind would deal with issues step by step in a logical sequence almost like a mathematical problem. Before deciding to act, a "normal" person would consider the consequences in ways that fairly accurately reflected reality. In contrast, thought processes in crowd members were simple, short-sighted, and not logical. Thoughts were more like dreams in which reality was distorted and ideas followed no logical sequence. At one moment a crowd member might be thinking about some enemy or scapegoat, then about an admired leader, then about loyalty to others in the crowd. Further, these thoughts were likely to be images (mental pictures) rather than abstractions. For example, national allegience would not be approached as an abstract ideal, but through a mental picture of a flag, or victorious armies.

Fourth, crowd members typically held important misconceptions about themselves and their environment. Leaders were commonly viewed as all-powerful, and crowd members themselves often had inflated notions of what they could accomplish. One consequence was that crowds could be controlled only by massive use of force. Feeling invincible, participants would ignore lesser measures.

Fifth, since crowds members believed their leaders to be invincible, a less than extraordinary performance by a leader could turn crowd adoration into hate. Having manufactured an imaginary, god-like figure, crowd members were unprepared to accept human fraility. Hence, LeBon characterized crowds as fickle.

It should be clear by now that LeBon had a rather unflattering view of the masses in general and crowds in particular. If common people were not animals already, crowds transformed them into animals. And LeBon did not stop with crowds. He extended his analysis to a variety of political forms where democratic decision-making was involved. Many of the processes subsumed under "Mental Unity of Crowds" were applied to popular elections, parliaments, and juries. Though he admitted that crowds were in some ways different from these more formal institutions, he argued that leaders could exercise the same sorts of demogogic tactics, that citizens acting in such groups were vulnerable to "suggestibility" and "contagion," and that the quality of decisions emerging from democratic bodies was inferior to those of earlier governmental forms (like monarchies). He especially warned against the use of secret ballot votes which he said paralled the anonymity of crowds. If people felt no one could identify them and their actions, customary social constraints were eliminated.

What are the weaknesses in LeBon's theory of collective behavior? (The reader might want to pause now and decide how much of LeBon's position should be accepted.)

1. Much of what LeBon claimed as explanation is really descriptive metaphor. Words like "contagion" do not unravel the cause of crowd behavior except possibly through analogy. Further, words like "suggestibility" though not metaphorical, explains very little upon close examination. If one grants that people in crowds behave alike (which will not be granted later), how much more do you know when such homogeneity is "explained" by suggestibility? Let's suppose one calls it "imitation": people in crowds are likely to imitate one another. Without far more detail on how "suggestibility" operates one could as easily call the homogeneity "imitation" and change nothing in the analysis. In short, LeBon has not really improved our understanding.

2. Some of LeBon's fundamental concepts have been debunked by modern science. "Hypnotism" as currently understood has nothing to do with crowd behavior. Similarly, there is nothing inferior about women and children! Further, many "savage" cultures have components far more sophisticated than the Western culture of LeBon's day (as well as our own).

3. LeBon's theory depended on leaders. Leaders were a *necessary condition* for crowds. Today we know that many, possibly even most, crowds materialized without leadership as LeBon meant the term. Read any account of street activities during American Civil Disorders and there will be no evidence of leaders. Hence, even if LeBon's theory has merit, it can only be applied to crowds where leadership is prominent.

4. LeBon inappropriately slipped between two levels of analysis; a level for individual crowd members, and the crowd as a whole. He constantly spoke of crowds believing certain things or behaving in certain ways. A crowd does not have a mind and hence cannot think! Nor can a crowd "act"! People in crowds can think and act, but the group as a distinct entity cannot. If LeBon wanted to characterize crowds, he should have developed concepts applicable to crowds instead of applying concepts appropriate soley to individuals.

5. The way LeBon described "contagion" provided no mechanism to explain how crowd behavior ever stops. If people are "suggestible" why don't they just continue to act? Obviously, crowds cease to exist, so somehow contagion is reversed. Further, why doesn't everyone near a crowd become involved? Are some people immune to the "contagion?"

6. LeBon failed to explain the ways in which societal conditions affect the types and intensity of specific instances of crowd behavior. If one grants that social conditions in France at the turn of the century were as LeBon described, why were some regions of the country and some time periods more likely to have rioting? Why did the crowd activity surrounding the demagogue Boulanger for example occur in July of 1886 and not before or after? If one wanted to apply LeBon's theory to American student unrest, why was the activity concentrated in the late sixties, and not before and after? In short, LeBon failed to link crowd action directly to social conditions in spite of his nearly hysterical emphasis on the political decay of France.

Since LeBon's work, social scientists have gathered much additional data on crowds. This data indicates the following:

a. Crowd members exercise far more rational thought than LeBon suggested. If, for example, crowd members are about to loot a store, they first look around for police.

b. There is often considerable division of labor within crowds. Not everyone is doing the same thing. In a lynch mob, for example, some people subdue the victim, some get the rope, some disarm local police, some act as lookouts, and so on. Hence, the homogeneity of behavior that LeBon decribed is inaccurate.

c. Crowd members participate for a variety of motives and under a variety of emotional states. Some are angry, some are excited, some are curious, some are greedy, some are seeking power, and so on. There is no evidence of emotional "contagion" which eliminates important individual differences in motives for participation.

Lest we be too severe, LeBon's work on collective behavior has some important strengths:

1. His belief that collective behavior can occur in other contexts than crowds is an important insight. The Congressional example in Chapter 1 was included to emphasize this point. Later, an approach to collective behavior will be presented which will add more plausibility to collective behavior in non-crowd situations.

2. His attempt to associate crowd behavior with conditions in the society has been widely imitated. Indeed, crowds often reflect societal tensions and can be part of important social movements.

3. His emphasis on the role of unconscious motives, though overstated, has added an important dimension to studies of crowds. In analyses of Southern lynch mobs, for example, one of the important factors seems to be unconscious fear among some whites of alleged sexual superiority of black males.

4. By drawing attention to crowds, LeBon opened up an important field for so-

cial scientists. His work indicated that human behavior in informal groups where activity is generated "spontaneously" is an important phenomenon to study.

In summary, LeBon asked many of the right questions, though his answers were largely incorrect. Few social scientists today accept his theories, but all trace the field of collective behavior back to *The Crowd.* Almost every modern theorist addresses questions originally raised by LeBon.

LeBon's influence on popular conceptions of crowds has also been great. Words like "contagion" and "suggestion" are part of "pop" social science, and after most any riot some "authority" or public official explains the disorder in terms of "mob psychology." Unfortunately, these misleading terms can have important political implications. By emphasising crowd irrationality, attention is directed away from societal conditions that may have caused the disorder and toward crowd participants who are characterized as either misguided, politically subversive, temporarily insane, or criminal. Hence, blame is attached only to rioters, while their grievances, and/or broader inequalities are ignored. Recall what was implied when President Nixon characterized anti-war demonstrators as "bums." If demonstrators were "bums," then their cause had no justification. The problem was the demonstrators, not the Vietnam war. Through history, people in power have found it politically expedient to impugn the integrity and motives of those who challenged their perogatives. LeBon's theory of collective behavior plays into the hands of the powerful.

THE CROWD AS A BIG FAMILY—SIGMUND FREUD

Sigmund Freud is clearly one of the most important and influential thinkers in Western history. Trained as a physician, he turned his intellect towards human maladies whose cause could not be related to biological illness. Much of his early work was done on "hysterics," people who despite apparent physical health had lost the ability to operate parts of their bodies. For example, some patients seemed unable to walk and showed all the superficial symptoms of paralysis. Yet their leg muscles did not atrophy, and under hypnosis the patients could be made to walk. Freud argued that their inability to walk was a result of some deep-seated mental anguish of which the patient was unaware but which affected behavior none the less. Further, the anguish was produced by real experiences which were so psychologically painful that the patient had "repressed" them into his/ her subconscious.[5] Freud found that if patients could only face these earlier experiences consciously, the neurotic symptoms (i.e., paralysis) would disappear.

The discovery of subconscious mental processes was of immense importance, but this was just the beginning. Through his long career, Freud developed a complex and subtle theory of human behavior and tried to apply it to a wide variety of human activity. His work was frequently controversial, especially when he based his "Psychoanalytic Theory" on human sexual motivation. Though "sexuality" was defined very broadly as a general instinct for life and self-preservation, many of its applications (e.g., describing breast feeding in sexual terms for both the mother and infant) were objectionable to Victorian Europe.

It would be impossible to summarize Freudian psychoanalytic theory here. To begin, several different theories are involved because Freud's views continued to evolve until his death (a mark of his ge-

nius). Further, his work is extremely complex, and almost any synopsis distorts it beyond recognition. Nevertheless, in order to examine his theory of crowd behavior, some groundwork must be laid. Rather than undertaking an inclusive summary, several key concepts will be described.

Probably one of the best overviews of psychoanalytic theory can be found in Ruth L. Munroe's *Schools of Psychoanalytic Thought*.[6] She stresses four major contributions of psychoanalytic theory which, though obvious today, were significant breakthroughs at the turn of the century.

First, Freud proposed the idea of "Psychological Determinism." No human behavior could be interpreted as "accidental"; rather, all human behavior was motivated. Many of the motives might be unconscious, but were effective forces nevertheless. Today we all are familiar with the notion of "Freudian Slip" where someone "mistakenly" says something which appears to be an error, but is what the person really feels deep down. This is one instance of "Psychological Determinism." Other examples can be found in persistent life patterns of people who seem to make the same mistakes over and over. They may know what is best, but continue to act contrary to their conscious interests. For instance, there are many cases of criminals who commit crimes

5. A wide variety of experiences could cause sufficient psychological pain to be forced from memory (i.e., repressed). For example, the death of a sibling or parent might be repressed. However, the severity of the actual event is not the only factor causing repression. The event frequently plays into a psychological predisposition, magnifying the impact of the occurrence. A child who secretly hopes for death of a parent will be especially affected by a parent's death.

6. Ruth L. Munroe *Schools of Psychoanalytic Thought*, (New York: Holt, Rinehart, and Winson, 1955).

in such careless ways as to invite capture. They will vehemently deny their wish to be caught, but always leave a trail of clues (like dropping their driver's license at the scene of the crime). In short, Freud argued that behind *every* action is a motive

Second, Freud elevated unconscious motivation to a prominent place in the determinants of human behavior. He did not deny an important role for conscious thought, but demonstrated that one might undertake actions through unrecognized motives. Today this is so widely accepted that it seems unnecessary to elaborate.

Third, not only was all human behavior motivated, but the motives are directed towards desirable goals and hence reflect what people *want* to occur. Thinking back to our example of the careless criminal who always gets caught, Freud would argue that this is precisely what the criminal was seeking. Or if a student always seems to oversleep and miss examinations, the carelessness may indicate a desire (probably unconscious) to flunk. The important point is that even actions which seem self-destructive and painful are based on a desire for that outcome.

Fourth, Freud emphasized a historical perspective in explanations of human motivation. Behavior at one point in time could not be thoroughly understood without recourse to a person's prior experiences. It was especially important to unravel childhood events to explain the behavior of adults, because during childhood crucial character traits were formed and especially powerful repression occurred. To understand our "careless" criminal his early psychological development would have to be examined.

With the above concepts in hand, we can now proceed to Freud's approach to crowd behavior. In the 1920's Freud read LeBon's work on crowds and was impressed with its descriptive content. He felt that LeBon had insightfully documented the way people behave in crowds, but argued that LeBon's *theory* was largely incorrect. In other words, he accepted LeBon's descriptions as empirically accurate while challenging his explanations.

In a short essay, "Group Psychology and the Analysis of the Ego"[7] Freud tried to apply psychoanalytic theory to the crowds which LeBon described. The essay includes some very complicated and sometimes vague ideas but has had considerable influence on the field of collective behavior.

Freud employed four related ideas to explain crowd behavior. All rest on psychoanalytic theory and really cannot be understood out of that context. First, Freud argued that people in crowds are in part seeking a return to infancy. Much of infancy is pleasurable and crowds (along with many other situations) provide an opportunity for adults to recapture these early experiences.

One such infantile joy involves a sense of strength actually based on weakness. While infants are almost powerless to directly control their environment, paradoxically, they often feel "omnipotent." When very young they cannot distinguish themselves from their environment and consequently feel at one with it. Unable to establish the boundaries of their own bodies, they are everything and everything is they. They don't know what a leg is, or an arm, or the crib or their mother and father and thus, the world is perceived as an undifferentiated mass with them at the center. This is a

7. See John Reckmon, (ed.) *A General Section from the Works of Sigmund Freud,* (Garden City, New Jersey: Doubleday, 1957).

difficult idea to get across but its importance can be seen in many facets of adult behavior. Most religions are founded on aspirations of attaining union with a superior being and the universe. For example, the Christian concept of communion involves establishing a oneness with Christ and hence with God and all creation. Similarly, many positive descriptions of experiences under the influence of hallucinogens such as LSD also involve attainment of a sense of unity with the universe. In one experiment when LSD was given to terminal cancer patients, some people near death were better able to accept their fate after a "trip" from which they gained a sense of their relationship to the "cosmic order of things." In short, as infants we all have the experience of feeling undifferentiated from our surroundings. Freud argued that subconsciously people often seek to return to this "omnipotent" state where the world is simple and we are its center.

Infancy has other desirable qualities. Freud argued that infants feel dependent and passive, for in reality little action is required of them, yet their needs are fulfilled. Parents feed, cloth, and nurture the infant while the infant has to do little in return. Though this conjures up images of decadent Roman nobles lying about on couches and being fed by obsequious slaves, it is a pleasurable experience which all infants undergo and has a very important implication. To be dependent, one has to be dependent on someone. In other words, somebody has to do the nurturing. This means that dependency can only be achieved when a parent-like figure is available.

Why are infantile omnipotence and dependency encouraged in crowds? Freud argued that people in crowds are seeking an omnipotent infantile state with the leader as a surrogate parent. One of the reasons crowd participants let themselves be controlled by a leader involves a subconscious need modeled on a former parental dependency. Omnipotence and dependency were pleasurable as an infant, and such are sought by adults.

A second mechanism which Freud used to explain crowd behavior involves the idea of "identification." Simply put, identification is an unconscious process through which an individual "pretends" to be someone else. Picture a boy of ten who aspires to be a big league baseball player. Let's say his idol is Johnny Bench and for several summers the youth tries to bat like Bench, throw like Bench, run like Bench, dress like Bench, and even picks up some of his speech mannerisms. Why does he do this? Freud would argue that in part the ten year old can achieve some of the excitement and fame of Bench's life through fantasy by putting himself in Bench's shoes as thoroughly as possible. Much day dreaming has similar intent.

Technically, identification does not involve "pretending." "Pretending" implies that the person really knows the fantasy is make-believe. As Freud uses the term, identification is unconscious and the person establishes bonds with his/her idol without awareness. However, the motive is usually the same (i.e., to experience in fantasy a variety of pleasures that are unavailable in real life).

When applying identification to crowds, Freud explained that bonds are established between the leader and the crowd members through identification. This is why it is important that the leader be authoritative and prestigious. Crowd members will be more likely to identify with a leader who seems powerful because more psychic rewards are possible. What fun is it to indulge in the fantasy of being a weak and unimportant person?

The third mechanism Freud used to explain crowd behavior is an extension of identification. After a crowd member has identified with the leader, the leader's perceived characteristics are taken inside, "introjected." It is not enough that the crowd members fantasize being the leader, they must replace some of their psychological characteristics with the leader's. In practice, Freud argued that crowd members disregard their own sense of right and wrong and take on what they perceive as the leader's morality. (Technically, their "ego ideal" and "super ego" are replaced with those of the leader.) Hence, inhibitions are altered and people will do anything consistent with their "new" morality. Freud used introjection to explain why people in crowds will behave differently than people in other contexts; how peaceful, law abiding citizens will take the law into their own hands and commit acts of violence for which they are later ashamed.

The fourth mechanism which Freud used to explain crowd behavior is by far the most confusing and the least plausible. He compared the crowd to a family and argued that crowd members identify with one another and generate substantial group unity (or *esprit de corps*). The explanation involved the notion of sibling rivalry, competition among children of the same family for the attention of their parents. Since no one child can monopolize parental nurturance, one way to reduce the rivalry is to develop a sense of unity in which the attention received by one child is somehow experienced by all. If the children identify with one another they can share in fantasy the attention received by others. Freud claimed

that similar processes occur in crowds. Crowd members identify with one another, building a sense of community and togetherness, as a way of sharing the attentions of the leader.

Now that Freud's theory of collective behavior has been summarized, it should be apparent that he thoroughly accepted LeBon's description of behavior in crowds. What has changed is its explanation: Freud provided a variety of theoretical mechanisms based on psychoanalytic insights. Probably most interesting is his application of these insights to crowd fickleness. Recall that LeBon claimed crowd members would at one moment be prepared to follow their leader anywhere, and at the next be screaming for his/her head. Freud explained this through "ambivalence" caused by the paradoxes of dependency. The price one must pay for being dependent is a restriction of freedom. If all rewards come from a leader, one is necessarily under his/her power. Though being nurtured is pleasurable, being controlled is not. Hence, crowd members may love a leader for the ability to reward and hate a leader for the ability to punish. These two feelings are in tension with one another, but as long as the leader provides suitable rewards the balance is tipped in favor of love. Once the leader ceases to reward crowd members, the scale is tipped rapidly towards hate and the leader may become the next victim of the crowd. There are other applications of Freud's theory to crowds. Unfortunately we do not have the space to go into them here. The curious reader should refer to Munroe's book or Freud's essay on crowds.

What are the weaknesses of Freud's approach to collective behavior? To begin, his work has many of the same vulnerabilities as LeBon's. The empirical data on which

Freud's work rests is largely inaccurate, and hence his theory falls victim to assumptions of crowd homogeneity, total irrationality, and the necessary presence of leaders. Recall that recent research shows crowd members do a variety of things for a variety of reasons, that they exercise considerable rational, conscious thought, and that prominent leaders may be the exception, not the rule. In addition, the central role which Freud develops for childhood experiences is probably a vast overstatement. There is no evidence that childhood experiences play a larger role in crowds than in other circumstances. Hence, his theory may be more an explanation of certain types of relations between leaders and followers (in a variety of contexts) than an explanation of behavior in crowds. Finally, psychoanalytic theory itself is the subject of considerable debate. Many prominent psychologists reject it entirely, while others accept only some of its components. Specifically, the concept of identification has come under wide attack, and other equally plausible mechanisms have been suggested which serve the same theoretical function.

But like LeBon, Freud's work on crowds has some merit. Where leaders do play a prominent role in crowds, Freud's insights have relevance. Few would deny a role for the subconscious, though its relative importance to other factors might be debated. Hence, Freud's major contribution to the social psychology of groups may be his partial explanations of leadership.

Probably more important than the details of a psychoanalytic explanation of crowds is the fact that someone as prominent as Freud considered crowds a worthy subject of study. By building on LeBon's work and providing a more plausible theoretical formulation, Freud stimulated important research. Unfortunately, his work, like LeBon's, plays into the hands of people who wish to divert attention from legitimate motives behind much collective behavior. If crowds can be explained through "father-figures" masquerading as leaders and the infantile fantasies of participants, there is no need to consider societal causes of the disorders. Student anti-war demonstrators may be viewed as "acting out" their psychological problems, and white policemen who "brutalize" black militants may be simply "compensating for their insecurities." Irrespective of whether either explanation has any truth, they ignore fundamental social pressures which may be far more important than any psychological explanation.

THE CROWD AS A HERD—HERBERT BLUMER

Approximately fifteen years passed between the time Freud recaste Gustave Le-Bon and the time Herbert Blumer turned his attention to collective behavior. During that interval, social scientists of various persuasions tried their hand at clarifying the field, only to restate the issues in new language which further served to confuse things.

Herbert Blumer was a sociologist doing significant work on a wide variety of social science problems. He viewed collective behavior as an important subfield, though its uniqueness was never specified in a compelling way. One reason for the fuzzy boundaries he proposed for the subfield was his attempt to include a wide variety of phenomena. Blumer linked the study of public opinion and social movements to crowds, while trying to show how all three were produced by tensions in the society. We will focus on his views of crowds which were defined in terms of people in face-to-face contact, engaged in relatively spontaneous and transitory activity outside of, or counter to, societal customs and norms. Basically, we will see how he explained the phenomena originally characterized by Le-Bon and Freud.

Unfortunately, Blumer, like Freud, took LeBon's description as given and then attempted to develop a plausible theory. Hence, his work necessarily rests on a weak empirical foundation. Nevertheless, Blumer's theoretical approach breaks significantly with LeBon and Freud, since he focused on the interactions *between participants* rather than the interactions between the leaders and followers. This was an important new insight, at least in emphasis.

While LeBon employed "hypnotism" and Freud "identification," Blumer developed the idea of "circular reaction." Circular Reaction was the crucial mechanism generating collective behavior, and Blumer described it as follows:

One gets a clue to the nature of elementary collective behavior by recognizing the form of social interaction that has been called *circular reaction*. This refers to a type of interstimulation wherein the response of one individual reproduces the stimulation that has come from another individual and in being reflected back to this individual reinforces the stimulation. Thus the interstimulation assumes a circular form in which the individuals reflect one another's state of feeling and in so doing intensifies this feeling. It is well evidenced in the transmission of feelings and moods among people who are in a state of excitement. One sees the process clearly amidst cattle in a state of alarm. The expression of fear through bellowing, breathing, and movements of the body, induces the same feeling in the case of other cattle who, as they in turn express their alarm, intensify this emotional state in one another. It is through such a process of circular reaction that there arises among cattle a general condition of intense fear and excitement as in the case of a stampede.

The nature of circular reaction can be further helpfully understood by contrasting it with in-terpretative interaction, which is the form chiefly to be found among human beings who are in association. Ordinarily human beings respond to one another, as in carrying on a conversation, by interpreting one another's actions or remarks and then reacting on the basis of the interpretation. Responses, consequently, are not made directly to the stimulation, but follow upon interpretation; further, they are likely to be different in nature from the stimulating acts, being essentially adjustments to these acts. Thus interpretative interaction might be likened to a game of tennis and has the character of a shuttle process instead of a circular process. It tends, in degree, to make people different; circular reaction tends to make people alike.[8]

It should be clear that Blumer's circular reaction is essentially a restatement of Le-Bon's idea of contagion, though Blumer provides a more detailed set of mechanisms. Circular reaction is not a medical metaphor and rests on the quality of interactions between peoples in crowds. Under "normal" circumstances communication involves extensive interpretation so that before reacting an individual exercises rational thought. In crowds, interpersonal responses are more like reflexes, and a chain reaction of activity can result.

With circular reaction as the foundation, Blumer proposed four steps in the formation of crowds. First, there must be a precipitating incident which catches the interest of people and draws them to the scene. Collective behavior will be facilitated if the

8. This passage can be found in A. McClung Lee, ed., *Principles of Sociology*, (New York: Barnes Noble Books, 1946). A useful excerpt of Blumer's work on Collective Behavior can be found in Robert R. Evans, (ed.), *Readings on Collective Behavior*, (Chicago: Rand McNally, 1969). The book has an excellent cross-section of articles, though most are too technical for a broad course in introductory sociology. Also much of the material is already dated and James F. Short and Marvin E. Wolfgang, (ed.), *Collective Violence*, (Chicago: Aldine, 1972) cited in Chapter 2 is a necessary supplement.

incident arouses impulses and feelings that heighten the emotions of potential participants.

Second, a "milling" process begins in which people move about and talk to one another. Each person's excitement is communicated to others and reflected back and forth among participants. This circular reaction stimulates passions and creates a common mood. Crowd members become more sensitive to one another and hence even more vulnerable to further stimulation.

Third, "collective excitement" develops which is a more intense stage of interaction and during which emotions become directed at a common object. Though the object may be the original precipitating incident, often attention is directed at a target for action. Hence, a common objective emerges providing unity and purpose for crowd members. For example, at My Lai that common objective might have been destruction of the village.

Finally, energies are focused on the objective, and people begin to implement actions consistent with their common goal. At this point, crowds begin to act on their impulses.

Blumer's theory of collective behavior provides an important insight by emphasizing the relations between crowd members. Clearly LeBon and Freud minimized this factor. Further, since leaders play little or no role in Blumer's formulation, his theory could have applicability for all crowds, not just those where leaders are prominent. Unfortunately, Blumer's work has serious weaknesses.

First, he accepts crowd homogeneity as empirically accurate. At the very least, he overstates similarities among crowd participants generated by circular reaction. Second, he assumes that rational thought pro-

cesses are virtually nonexistent in crowds. Recent research has refuted that view. Third, if circular reaction produces the irrational homogeneity he claims, how can one explain that crowds frequently change their focus of attention (and targets) and that crowd behavior eventually stops? Anti-war demonstrators may begin by listening to speeches, then vandalize an ROTC building, then march to the University President's house, and then stage a sit-in. Rudé describes bread riots as a sequence of events which could start at a local bakery shop, move to a massive street demonstration, then generate a list of grievances sent to a local magistrate. Finally, circular reaction is at best empirically unsubstantiated. There is no evidence that interpretative processes are suspended in crowds or that participants respond in a reflex manner to "stimulation." The analogy to herds of stampeding cattle is very misleading and plays into the hands of people who wish to dismiss the legitimate grievances that many crowds reflect.

SUMMARY AND CONCLUSIONS

The three theories of collective behavior described in this chapter all emphasize how people gathered together can be transformed from peaceful law abiding citizens to a uniform mass, swayed by passion and unable to exercise even the most elementary forms of rationality. Despite different explanatory mechanisms all three theories are essentially theories of contagion. Sociologist Ralph Turner, describes contagion theories as follows: "The foremost problem which this type of theory sets for the investigator is to explain how people in collectivities come to behave (a) uniformly, (b) intensely, and (c) at variance with their usual patterns."[9]

9. From "Collective Behavior" by Ralph H. Turner in *Handbook of Modern Sociology*, ed. Robert E. L. Faris, 1964. Reprinted by permission of Rand McNally College Publishing Co.
This article is an excellent review of the literature up to the early sixties, but probably too difficult for most undergraduates.

As each theory was presented, weaknesses and strengths were highlighted. Turner argues that all contagion theories have five basic flaws, and these will serve as a useful summary of weaknesses with the contagion approach.

1. There is no compelling evidence for anything approximating contagion. For example, it is not true that crowd bystanders are automatically swept up in the passions of the crowd.

2. There is no compelling evidence that one needs a special theory for the psychological processes of people in crowds as distinct from the psychological processes of people in other sorts of groups. Social science has shown that we all are constantly influenced by those around us whether the group is a crowd, a family, a business, or an audience. If crowds differ from these other aggregates, it is at most a question of degree, not kind.

3. All of the mechanisms proposed by contagion theorists to explain crowd development (hypnotism, identification, circular reaction, etc.) resist empirical verification. And where similar mechanisms have been unearthed, they are not in crowd situations. For example, the most plausible case for identification can be made in long lasting family relationships (like between parents and children), and even here there is much debate.

4. Contagion theory provides no explanation for shifts in crowd activity or its termination. In fact, crowds can alter their course and eventually do distintegrate.

5. Contagion theory cannot explain the "division of labor" within a crowd. Not all people do the same thing or have the same motives, and these distinctions are crucial. They may ultimately hold the key to explanations of behavior in crowds. We shall return to this issue in later chapters.

In summary, contagion theory is unsatisfactory. The important question, then, is how much longer it can be used as a political tool on a gullible public.

Before moving on to other issues, there is another body of theory in the same tradition which warrants brief mention. Typically it is less well formulated than contagion theory and hence, does not deserve extensive consideration. Recall that LeBon explained crowds not only in terms of contagion, but through the types of people who were likely to participate. While almost anyone might be caught up in a crowd, particularly susceptible were rootless urban masses and their "nervous," "excitable" leaders. In essence, LeBon was saying that crowds tend to draw people with predispositions towards irrationality and violence. Turner has called this explanation of collective behavior "convergence" theory.

"For investigators employing this kind of theory, the problem of identifying a mechanism and specifying conditions under which contagion will create a homogeneous crowd out of a heterogeneous aggregate evaporates, as the produce of a faulty assumption. The problems instead become those of identifying relevant latent tendencies in masses of people, the circumstances that will bring people with similar latencies together, and the kinds of events which will tigger these tendencies."[10]

Turner identifies three types of explanations in the convergence tradition. First, some theories try to explain collective behavior in terms of "outsiders" who have similar latent tendencies that are released in crowds. For example, one might explain a brawl at a high school dance by blaming teenagers from another part of town who crashed the party and created the trouble. Second, some convergence theories emphasize the role of people who by nature are more susceptible to irrational and violent behavior. The "riff-raff" theory of Civil Disorders, for instance, blamed the Watts (Los Angeles) riot, on a small portion of the black community with little education, criminal records, and no steady job. Third, a more sophisticated approach has emphasized the latent pathology in all people: a common "hang-up" perspective. For example, Dollard, Doob, Miller, Mowrer, and Sears (1939) explained the incidence of lynching in the South in terms of frustration among poor whites over repressed economic conditions. Accumulated frustrations produced hostility eventually directed at an available and relatively safe target; blacks accused of indiscretion.[11]

10. Turner, "Collective Behavior," p. 387.
11. John Dollard et al., *Frustration and Aggression*, (New Haven, Conn.: Yale University Press, 1939). We will examine this work more carefully later when the "Frustration Aggression Hypothesis" is examined.

Convergence theory, like contagion theory cannot explain shifts in crowd behavior or the different roles people acquire in crowds. Similarly, it rests on an assumption of homogeneous motives which has not received empirical support. Finally it addresses only the intensity of crowd behavior and not its target. While the convergence theory proports to explain how homogeneous, impassioned, group behavior involves the release of latent pathological needs, there are no mechanisms describing how the motives are acted upon. For example, even if it were true that Civil Disorders were caused by "riff-raff," why did they attack inner city stores and police and not schools, government buildings, factories, and white residential neighborhoods? An explanation for this curious selection of riot targets requires mechanisms not considered by convergence theory.

In conclusion, the traditional approaches to collective behavior, though popular with the media, government officials, and the general public, have little merit. Fortunately, social scientists have moved well beyond these earlier theories and we turn to this more sophisticated work shortly.

For Further Reading

Evans, Robert R. ed. *Readings in Collective Behavior*. Chicago: Rand McNally, 1969.

Provides interesting excerpts from the works of many of the people discussed in this book.

Turner, Ralph H. "Collective Behavior" in *Handbook of Modern Sociology*. ed. Robert E. Faris Chicago: Rand McNally, 1964.

Presents a far more thorough discussion of the early writers mentioned in this book, but is probably too difficult for most undergraduates.

4 | Societal Causes of Collective Behavior– Kornhauser, Smelser and Related Perspectives

THE traditional views of collective behavior described in the preceding chapter emphasized events at the scene of crowd activity. Societal causes were largely ignored, though LeBon spoke about a general weakening of the social order. In this chapter, some attempts to link collective behavior to larger social conditions will be discussed.

There have been far more analyses of factors predisposing societies to collective behavior than studies of crowds *per se*. Much of the work actually addresses a broader question: How can one explain the overall levels of collective violence in a society? Included as "collective violence" are riots, rebellions, *coups d'etat*, civil wars, and revolutions. And within each of these categories are typically several sub-types. We shall first confine our attention to factors most closely connected to the more spontaneous and transitory forms, and then limit ourselves to a few of the more well-known approaches in this body of collective behavior analyses.

Even though this chapter ignores a vast amount of material, our discussion must be further simplified. A thorough presentation would involve far too many pages and would require a rather sophisticated foundation in several different social sciences.

Hence, this chapter represents just the tip of the iceburg, and a smaller tip than found in other chapters.

COLLECTIVE BEHAVIOR AND MASS SOCIETY— KORNHAUSER

When LeBon spoke of the disintegration of French society he emphasized two factors; internal rot within the government, and growing power of the uneducated, rootless masses. Many theorists have picked up these themes and refined their concepts and mechanisms. Writing in the late 1950's, William Kornhauser formulated a particularly well-known and influential version of this "mass society" theory, and provided some important insights into the causes of collective behavior.

Just as LeBon reacted to reverberations of France's industrialization, social scientists like Kornhauser reacted to the disruptive events of the mid-twentieth century. During the 1950's, Western thinkers were intensely concerned with societal conditions which earlier had spawned totalitarian regimes in Germany, Spain, Italy, Japan, and the Soviet Union. The scholarly interest was more than academic; they hoped to learn enough to prevent similar developments in the future. Hence, Kornhauser and others were seeking totalitarian antidotes in the "cold war" years which followed the tragedies of World War II. One of the resulting biases of work in this period was a type of chauvanism in which American democracy was depicted as an ideal towards which all nations should aspire. Too often this encouraged naive analyses of American society which contained unwarranted pejorative descriptions of dissidents.

For our purposes, Kornhauser's main insights concern societal conditions which produce collective behavior. He argued that when nations become "mass societies" they are especially prone to wide-spread unrest. The concept of "mass society" refers to a type of national disintegration similar to what LeBon described and is contrasted with three other kinds of societies (in a two-by-two table presented below) less likely to experience collective behavior.[1]

Availability of Non-Elites

		low	high
Accessibility of Elites	**low**	Communal Societies	Totalitarian Societies
	high	Pluralist Societies	Mass Societies

From Kornhauser, 1953

The vertical dimension, "Accessibility of Elites" involves the degree to which the people in power can be influenced by citizens in their society. For example, in medieval societies people belonged to classes which prevented commoners from having much impact on nobles and the monarch. Peasants "knew their place" and there were no formal provisions by which they might participate in their governments. Elections, petitions, lobbying, and other democratic forms of activity were nonexistent. In contrast, Western democracies provide a number of ways for citizens to make their demands felt. For instance, Kornhauser argued that the United States had accessible elites and that its representative form of government made public officials accountable to citizens.

The horizontal dimension, "Availability of Non-Elites," is a bit more difficult to understand. Its structural manifestations (i.e., the characteristics of a society as a whole) are seen in the number and variety of groups and organizations to which people belong. For example, a medieval peasant was attached to his family, his manor, his religion, and possibly a fraternity or guild. These groups provided certain satisfactions and an anchor for his life which gave him values and rules for behavior. In modern democratic societies people are attached to

1. For those unfamiliar with tabular presentations, an explanation is needed. A simple example is perhaps the best way to proceed. Let's suppose you wanted to describe alcoholic beverages. Two dimensions come to mind: whether or not the beverage is distilled, and whether the beverage is made from grain (like wheat) or a fruit (like grapes). Note that each dimension has two categories (distilled vs. not distilled, and grain base vs. fruit base). We can use the two dichotomous dimensions to construct a table describing types of alcoholic beverages in summary form.

Source of the Beverage

		Grain	Fruit
Manufacturing Process	**Distilled**	whisky	liqueur
	Not Distilled	beer	wine

The table is interpreted as follows. Each square in the table represents the combination of one category from each of the two dimensions. For example, alcoholic beverages which are distilled from grain are whiskies. Alcoholic beverages which are made from grain but not distilled are beers. And so on. The point of such tables is to efficiently summarize concepts based on two dichotomous dimensions.

families, political organizations, religious groups, and voluntary associations. Again these provide a sense of reality and boundaries for behavior. In contrast, some societies lack autonomous groups, and citizens are set adrift with few constraints on their behavior. They feel "atomized" and "alienated." They experience a sense of distrust, powerlessness, and loneliness. In short, like small children separated from their parents, when groups and organizations disappear from a society, (even temporarily) people feel lost. Without such ties citizens are easily recruited to "extremist" causes or any actions which promise an immediate remedy for their problems. Hence, they are "available."

Kornhauser characterized mass society as the combination of highly accessible elites and highly available non-elites. More specifically, elites are vulnerable to pressure while citizens are cast adrift because the groups which held their allegiance and provided them with a sense of belonging are largely missing. The absence of independent organizations also means that there are no buffers between masses and elites. For example, the Congress of the United States acts as a useful barrier between citizens and the president since between elections popular wishes can formally affect the president only through laws passed by the Senate and House. Theoretically, the president is accessible, but *not directly and immediately*. In contrast, mass societies are characterized by a lack of mediating structures so that the whims of restless atomized citizens can be quickly and powerfully directed at their leaders. Russia immediately prior to its revolution and Germany in the the 1920's would be examples of mass societies. (According to Kornhauser)

Note however, that, "not all members of a society, *but only People in the mass* (italics, Kornhauser's) are disposed to seize the opportunity provided in all spheres of society, and to do so in an unrestrained manner. This is true for two reasons. First, when large numbers of people are interrelated only as members of a mass, they are more likely to pressure elites to provide satisfactions previously supplied by a plurality of more proximate groups. Second, they are likely to do so in a direct and unmediated way, because there is a paucity of intervening groups to channel and filter popular participation in the larger society. As a result, mass participation tends to be irrational and unrestrained, since there are few points at which it may be checked by personal experience and the experiences of others. Where people are not securely related to a plurality of independent groups, they are available for all kinds of adventures and activist modes of intervention in the larger society. It is one thing for a population to participate at specified times and institutional ways for defined interests— for example, through trade associations and trade unions, or in elections. It is quite another to creat *ad hoc* methods of direct pressure on critical centers of society, such as "invasion" of a state legislature, street political gangs, etc."[2]

It is important to emphasize that Kornhauser is not just trying to explain why some societies are more likely to experience crowd behavior, but to explain the occurrence of a wide range of related activity including recruitment to extremist social movements. Hence, his interests are much broader than most collective behavior theorists and this leads to some problems. We will discuss these problems shortly.

Why are the other three kinds of societies unlikely to have collective behavior? Though pluralist societies have accessible elites, citizens are attached to a variety of groups. Consequently, the public is less sus-

2. Reprinted with permission of Macmillan Publishing Co., Inc. From *The Politics of Mass Society* by William Kornhauser © The Free Press, a Corperation, 1959, pp. 37-38.

ceptible to impetuous, irrational activity and elites are buffered from public demands. In other words, non-elites are *not* available. Totalitarian societies have available non-elites because *independent* mediating organizations have been eliminated (e.g., labor unions may exist but are controlled by the state). However, since harsh political measures keep the masses from pressuring leaders, elites are *not* accessible. Finally, communal societies have *neither* accessible elites *nor* available non-elites, therefore popular pressures on rulers are theoretically unlikely.

In this brief summary of Kornhauser's positions some unfortunate simplification has been necessary. Yet, taking this into account, there are still certain obvious problems with Kornhauser's theory as an explanation of collective behavior.

First, his four-fold typology of societies is too simple and ignores a variety of important dimensions. For example, nowhere is there any mention of the way specific, concrete hardships affect the masses. People often take to the streets because they are hungry, not simply because their "alienation" makes them easy recruits for some demagogue. Also absent are considerations of social inequality and injustice. One could argue that societies with large segments of their population in subordinate positions should have substantial unrest, although the factors suggested by Kornhauser might affect the form of unrest.

Second, by resting his theory on the psychological variable of "alienation" (and related mental states) Kornhauser leaves no room for consideration of collective behavior as a *rational, instrumental* activity implemented by psychologically *stable* citizens. Why must people feel rootless in order to take to the streets? Before the Nazi take-over, citizens in Germany experienced a severe economic depression under a government unable to improve their lot. They may have been "alienated," but support for Hitler probably had as much to do with promises of food and shelter as appeals to a psychological malaise.

Third, Kornhauser's theory tries to explain such a wide variety of social unrest that many important distinctions are ignored. His work is best viewed as an explanation of vulnerability to totalitarian appeals, and not as an explanation of crowd behavior *per se*. Since crowds can reflect a variety of motives under many different social conditions, Kornhauser's brush strokes are too broad for our purposes.

Fourth, Kornhauser's theory operates at the societal (or national) unit of analysis. This may have some utility in explaining the amount and intensity of unrest in nations, but is ineffective for unraveling the cases of a *particular instance* of collective behavior or different *rates* of unrest among people of different classes *within* a given country. For example, Kornhauser has little to say about American Civil Disorders involving inner city areas and black people. Why was it primarily blacks who rioted? And why only urban blacks? His mass society theory might apply to the United States as a whole but it says little about different groups of people within the country.

Finally, Kornhauser focuses only on collective violence undertaken by citizens. What about collective violence by the police and the military? Kornhauser explicitly places these kinds of events outside his immediate interest. Yet, this implies that only the common people can engage in impulsive, irrational crowd behavior. My Lai is an incident of collective violence that would not be considered by Kornhauser.

In summary, Kornhauser's approach to collective behavior once again raises the spectre of LeBon. Kornhauser is a bit more charitable: collective behavior participants are almost innocent victims of their mass society and ruthless demagogues. Yet, crowd members are viewed as creatures of passion swept up in the excitement of events, lacking concrete social grievances. Like LeBon's work, Kornhauser's plays into the hands of people who seek to minimize any legitimate challenge to social order.

COLLECTIVE BEHAVIOR AND SOCIAL STRAIN— NEIL SMELSER

Neil Smelser's major work on collective behavior was published shortly after Kornhauser's *The Politics of Mass Society*. It reflects many of the same underlying issues, though it is much more focused on crowds *per se*. Smelser hoped to produce a theory that could link societal characteristics with *specific* instances of collective behavior without limiting the explanation to incidence or intensity at a societal level.

Smelser's *Theory of Collective Behavior* rests heavily (one might say ponderously) on Talcot Parson's Social Action Theory, a broad systematic set of typologies which attempts to abstract the essence of human activity. Parson's work is extremely complex and has been the target of much valid criticism. Fortunately, one can understand the thrust of Smelser's work without direct recourse to Parsonian Social Action Theory.

Even excluding the Parsonian framework, summarizing Smelser's theory of collective behavior is extremely difficult. His approach is complicated and sometimes is presented ambiguously. Hence, any brief overview will do his ideas some injustice.

Smelser begins by providing a general framework in which to place the details of his theory. He borrows the "value added" model from economics; this involves a description of the way manufactured goods acquire increasing economic worth as they are transformed from raw materials to a final product. For example, a kitchen stove begins as iron ore, the ore is refined, steel produced, the steel is shaped into parts for a stove, the parts are covered with baked enamel, and finally the stove is assembled. At each step the value of the original iron is increased so that iron ore valued at, say, $20, is eventually sold to retail stores as a stove worth $200. Clearly, the manufacturing process adds value to the iron ore. (Hence the term "value-added.") In addition, at each stage the uses to which the product can be put are reduced; iron ore could be used to manufacture any iron or steel product. Once the ore has become steel it cannot be used for cast iron goods. Once the steel is shaped into parts for a stove it cannot be used to build an automobile. One can think of the process as a large funnel where the variety of product applications becomes more narrow as its refinement continues.

What does this have to do with crowds? Smelser uses the value added model to explain how broad societal conditions (at the wide part of the funnel) are increasingly transformed into more specific manifestations which eventually result in a collective behavior incident (at the narrow part of the funnel.) At each step, the range of possible outcomes is reduced and the probability of collective behavior is increased. There are six proposed stages in this process.

1. Structural Conduciveness—structural conduciveness involves the presence of the elements which eventually produce a collective behavior incident. For example, one could not have a race riot if a commu-

nity did not have two races in close proximity to one another. Or, police could not attack demonstrators where there are no people ready to demonstrate or police assigned to the task of controlling them. This is analogous to the iron ore in stove manufacturing. In essence, structural conduciveness represents the raw material for collective behavior.

2. Structural Strain—Structural strain describes contradictions or tensions between basic elements of a society. For example, in American society law is supposed to be equally applied to all citizens: in sociological language, laws are supposed to applied universalistically. On the other hand, laws are also supposed to be applied with some consideration for the circumstances surrounding the alleged offence. We would prefer to see a policemen reprimand, but not arrest, a college student whose first contact with crime involved getting drunk and breaking some windows at a fraternity party. In contrast, were this college student an habitual trouble-maker who got his kicks by fighting and destroying property, some kind of official intervention would be desired. Hence, the policeman is in a bind. Does he arrest all vandals as the law literally requires, or does he use judgment in applying the law differently according to the circumstances? In so far as this *contradiction* is built into our entire system of criminal justice, there is structural strain. Two fundamental values in the society are in opposition.

Unfortunately, Smelser is never clear on whether structural strain reflects objective conditions in the society or the perception of those conditions by its citizens. For our purposes it will not distort his approach too much if we assume that structural strain concerns the perception of contradictions in

the society. More specifically, structural strain reflects a poor fit between what people think should happen and what actually does. In the case of the college vandal, structural strain could be an awareness that the vandal was arrested though he never had been in trouble before. Here, structural strain is produced by the contradiction between a belief that laws should be applied flexibly and the student's arrest.

At this point a minor complication must be introduced. Smelser included panics, crazes, hostile outbursts, and social movements under the collective behavior label. Panics involve crowds fleeing a particular situation; the proverbial fire in a crowded theater is a good example. Crazes involve groups (not necessarily in face-to-face contact) whose primary motive is self-expression, or letting off steam. Example include religious revial meetings, cheering crowds at football games, or societal fads like Davy Crockett coonskin hats, hoola-hoops, and more recently, longer hair on men. Hostile outbursts are violent crowds (e.g., riots); participants are undertaking some action as a group to directly affect the causes of structural strain. For example, a lynch mob is a hostile outburst because the actions are not flight, nor sheer expression (though that may be also occurring) but an attempt to remedy a perceived problem. Finally, social movements involve the transformation of reactions to structural strain into relatively permanent organizational forms. For instance, in a case where dissatisfaction with working conditions might lead to the establishment of labor unions, a social movement has evolved. Note that structural strain is a precondition of all these forms of "collective behavior," though we will be most interested in panics, expressive crowds, and hostile outbursts.

In addressing the conditions facilitating a "hostile outburst" (i.e., collective violence), Smelser further specifies three factors which increase the chances that structural strain will be perceived. Firestone (1971) summarizes these as follows.

It must be possible to "identify", in the sense of subjective perceptions, the agents responsible for the strain. Channels for expressing grievances must be largely absent. Lastly, the material environment of the situation must facilitate: a) communication among the aggrieved, b) accessibility of the objects to be attacked, and c) spatial circumstances allowing the necessary physical actions to occur.[3]

In other words, people must be able to decide who's responsible, be unable to get satisfaction through normal procedures, and be gathered near their intended target.

3. Generalized Belief—Generalized beliefs are psychological states which evolve in response to ambiguities created by social strain. The social strain creates a situation with which people are unfamiliar, and therefore no habitual response is forthcoming. Generalized beliefs act to interpret this condition. Further, generalized beliefs form the cornerstone of Smelser's theory of collective behavior. It is generalized beliefs which distinguish collective behavior from other kinds of group activity. In fact

...We shall define collective behavior as *mobilization on a basis of a belief which redefines social action.* . . . These beliefs differ, however, from those which guide many other types of behavior. They involve a belief in the existence of extraordinary forces—threats, conspiracies, etc.—which are at work in the universe. They also involve an assessment of extraordinary consequences which follow if collective attempts to reconstitute social action are successful. These are the beliefs on which collective behavior is based, (we shall call them *generalized beliefs*) and are thus akin to magical beliefs.[4]

How do these generalized beliefs operate?

Before collective action can be taken to reconstitute the situation brought about by structural strain, this situation must be made meaningful to potential actors. This meaning is supplied in generalized belief which identifies the source of strain, attributes certain characteristics to the source, and specifies certain responses to the strain as possible or appropriate.[5]

In the specific case of hostile outbursts (e.g., riots), the strain produces confusion and anxiety which leads to three common reactions in potential rioters. Specific agents are identified who are seen responsible for the strain, aggression is channeled towards those agents, and increased feelings of power and competence give crowd members the sense that they can exert important influence on the source of the strain. However, Smelser emphasizes that these beliefs are simplistic, "shortcircuits" of reality. Crowd members have reduced complex societal questions which operate at various levels of aggregation to naive and inaccurate misunderstanding. For example, were a group of college students to "liberate" a dean's office in a desire to end the Vietnam War, Smelser might characterize this activity as misguided, dicated by a generalized belief. To think that taking over a deans office would affect American foreign policy would be naive and simplistic.

To summarize, Smelser *defines* collective behavior in terms of generalized belief.

3. Joseph M. Firestone, "Three Frameworks for the Study of Violence: A Critique and Some Suggestions for a New Synthesis", Mimeo, Center for Comparative Political Research, SUNY, Binghamton, 1971.
4. Reprinted with permission of Macmillan Publishing Co., Inc. From *Theory of Collective Behavior*, by Neil Smelser. © Neil J. Smelser, 1963, p. 8.
5. Smelser, *Theory of Collective Behavior*, p. 16.

When social strain generates a situation which is ambiguous, potential crowd members produce *a common belief* about the strain. This belief becomes the dominant motive for all by explaining the situation and suggesting appropriate action. Characteristically, the generalized belief is an inaccurate and naive assessment, suggesting simplistic remedies for complex problems. Further, people operating in other contexts, as individuals or in institutions, function by the use of beliefs which more intelligently account for complexity.

Hopefully, the reader has noted yet another resurrection of Gustave LeBon. Like the famous count from Transylvania, he keeps coming back from the grave. Once more, the mental processes of crowd participants are described as irrational, thus belittling their motives. After all, if crowds are motivated by generalized beliefs which are simplistic, naive, and "short-circuits" of reality, there is no reason to take their messages seriously.

4. Precipitating Factors—Blumer talked about a similar phenomenon: a specific, concrete event calling attention to a generalized belief or dramatizing its importance. In the case of the Newark Civil Disorder, the precipitating event was the arrest of a black cab driver. The incident called attention to police brutality and larger oppressions by white society.

5. Mobilization—mobilization involves the gathering of people at a given location, often the scene of the precipitating event. At this point, Smelser discusses potential roles for leaders, the composition of the crowd, and its physical surroundings. Unfortunately, he really adds little to LeBon's insights on these issues, although his presentation is more cogent. Far more productive is an article by McPhail and Miller on the

assembling process (1973) in which mobilization is explained by the availability of information about a collective behavior opportunity, ease of access to the scene, and an absence of competing activities. In other words, mobilization is treated as a series of conscious choices by individuals which depend on factors much like one would consider under "normal" circumstances. A potential rioter must learn about a possible rewarding activity, find out its location, be able to get to the scene, and, and not be side tracked along the way.[6]

6. Social Control—If collective behavior takes the form of a hostile outburst, the application of counterforce must be considered. For collective behavior involving flight, (like in a panic during a theatre fire,) or expressive behavior which does not disrupt the public order (like a revival meeting), the application of counterforce is irrelevant. When force is employed, Smelser recommends

a) prevent communication in general so that beliefs cannot be disseminated. b) prevent interaction between leaders and followers, so that mobilization is difficult. c) refrain from taking a conditional attitude towards violence by bluffing or vacilating in the use of the ultimate weapon of force. d) refrain from entering the issues and controversies that move the crowd; remain impartial, unyielding, and fixed on the principle of maintaining law and order."[7]

Getting back to the idea of a value added approach in Smelser's model, notice how the funnel was narrowed at each step. As each stage was passed, fewer and fewer outcomes were possible. Finally, when the

6. Clark McPhail and David Miller, "The Assembling Process: A Theoretical and Empirical Examination," *ASR*, December, 1973.
7. Smelser, *Theory of Collective Behavior,* p. 267.

crowd is mobilized and gathered at one location, nothing but the forces of law and order stand between the crowd and its goals. If these forces are ineffective, the only result is a hostile outburst. In the case of expressive crowds seeking to "let off steam", Smelser claims social control is largely irrelevant since it is likely that the behavior will be allowed to proceed.

Let's undertake a brief, not-so-instant replay of the Detroit race riot of 1943 to see how Smelser's scheme might be applied.[8] As a result of World War II many blacks from the South sought work in Detroit's booming industries. Of course, Detroit was primarily white at the time. The influx of new workers, coupled with limited production of homes (production was aimed at war needs), created a housing shortage. In addition, many blacks were prepared to work for relatively low wages. All these factors can be summarized through the concept of structural conduciveness. Structural strain developed as blacks began to compete with whites for jobs and housing. Both races felt themselves threatened. Tension mounted and in most attempts to deal with the situation, demeaning racial stereotypes were used as prominent characterizations. Smelser would probably label these views "generalized beliefs." One weekend afternoon white and black teenagers got into a brawl at a local beach, and rumors of severe injury spread through both white and black neighborhoods. With this as the precipitating incident, crowds rushed towards the beach (mobilization) and interracial fighting followed. Law enforcement personnel were unable to control the situation and a major race riot occurred. Many people were injured and several deaths (mostly blacks) resulted.

The example demonstrates that Smelser's approach to collective behavior has considerable plausibility. However, it also contains substantial problems. First, the concept of structural strain needs considerable elaboration. As it stands, almost anything can qualify as structural strain. A crucial attribute of any theory is that its explanatory mechanisms be able to separate very important factors from moderately important factors, from unimportant factors. For example, if an individual cannot get along with people one might "explain" his behavior by saying he has personality problems. If an individual gets very nervous before an exam and "chokes", one might also say he has personality problems. If an individual gets hostile when drinking one might again say he has personality problems. Obviously, attributing the behavior in each case to "personality problems" is not very useful since "personality problems", though seemingly an important factor, is a term too loosely employed to explain very much. If almost any behavior can be caused by personality factors it is not a very powerful theoretical concept. Smelser's structural strain has a similar weakness. Since all societies have substantial strain, it cannot be a useful predictor of the likelihood of riots. As one would need a more thoroughly elaborated view of personality, one needs a more

8. A few new definitions might be helpful here. A "Civil Disorder" involves property crimes and collective violence between people of one race and the *institutional representatives* of the larger society (like retail merchants and police). A "Southern style race riot" is collective behavior in which bands of the politically dominant race act aggressively against passive members of the politically subordinate race. For example, white citizens might rampage through black neighborhoods while blacks put up almost no resistance. A "Northern style race riot" involves collective violence with both races participating aggressively. The 1943 Detroit Race Riot was of the Northern variety.

complex notion of structural strain in order to make meaningful distinctions useful in explaining collective behavior.

Second, a detailed examination of structural strain unearths other difficulties. One of the most telling is Smelser's assumption that if channels for the communication of grievances are open, strain will not develop and hostile outbursts will not occur. Recall that when Kornhauser's work was described, it was noted that many American social scientists of the 50s had a somewhat naive and overly flattering view of democracy in the United States. (I am tempted to call this view a "generalized belief.") Smelser seems to share the same bias: he assumes that communication is all one needs in order to remedy grivances. He ignores (a) that one's message may be misunderstood, (b) that one may communicate and no one may choose to respond, and (c) that one may communicate and no one may be allowed to respond. For example, during the late 60s many students had the experience of endless meetings with university administrators where all parties were communicating like crazy. Typically, this generated position papers, memoranda, and more meetings. Often little was done to respond concretely to student grievances. Indeed, the meetings, allegedly called to foster communication, were frequently attempts to stall students—wait them out. Blacks have had similar experiences with riot commissions. They communicated at great length about the problems of being black and poor in America, but conditions remained largely unchanged. Hence, Smelser fails to recognize that people may understand the grievances of a particular group but choose not to respond. They have "other fish to fry."

Third, the concept of generalized belief has severe problems. To begin, Smelser claims that the generalized belief is the *dominant* motive of crowd participants. In other words, the crowd is rather homogeneous in its perception of the situation and resulting motives. However, there is no compelling evidence for this position. Indeed, the evidence suggests a diversity of motives within any given individual and within the crowd as a whole. More fundamentally, Smelser never specifies how *dominant* the generalized belief is supposed to be. It is the *only* belief about the situation held by crowd members? Is it the only *conscious* belief held by crowd members? Is it one of several beliefs, but the *most important?* Is it one of several beliefs, but *only one held in common?* Is it *just one of several* important beliefs? And so on. In short, we are never told how dominant is dominant. Equally honorable and talented social scientists could look at the same crowd and never agree whether or not a generalized belief was present. One investigator might say there was no generalized belief since the crowd members had several motives. Another might agree that several motives existed, but argue that since fifty percent (for example) of the crowd had one salient belief, generalized belief was present. A third might contend that fifty percent was not enough, and seventy-five percent must have the same salient belief if generalized belief is to be operative. All might agree that fifty percent of the crowd shared the same important motive, yet disagree whether a generalized belief existed.

Another problem with generalized belief involves its characterization as naive, magical, and a "short-circuit" of reality. Who's to say what's a magical belief and what isn't? To judge a belief one must have an accurate picture of the situation as a yardstick In most circumstances, no completely "accurate" picture exists, or at least no picture about which everyone would agree. For example, for several consecutive falls and springs thousands of antiwar demonstrators turned out in Washington D.C.. Many knowledgeable people claimed that such demonstrations were a waste of time since the Administration was not taking them seriously. At most, the demonstrations were a temporary nuisance for local police, but an insignificant influence on national policy. Therefore, people who thought the Administration was really concerned about the demonstrations were supposedly operating under rather naive evaluations of the situation.

Now we learn that the Nixon regime was in near hysteria over the demonstrations, and that massive spying operations were implemented against citizens of political persuasions judged unacceptable by the Administration. Further, the White House believed substantial numbers of these demonstrations were directed and financed by foreign governments and persisted in these beliefs even after the FBI and CIA delivered assurances that such was not the case. Unsatisfied with assessments of the two leading security agencies in the United States, the President and his staff set up their own secret surveillance operation to keep tabs on dissidents. Who, then, was dominated by naive, magical beliefs? The demonstrators were actually being taken most seriously by the Administration, and if anything, it was the White House which was misperceiving the situation. The moral should be obvious. It is often not clear what an accurate perception of any given situation should be. Hence, it is usually impossible to tell when a belief is magical and naive.

A final problem with generalized belief involves Smelser's assertion that the beliefs of crowd members are fundamentally different from the beliefs of people in other circumstances. Given the difficulties in assessing a generalized belief, a comparison between beliefs of crowd members and those of other people is problematic. In addition, the evidence which does exist has not uncovered the differences postulated by Smelser. Think back to the example just described.

In conclusion, Smelser took an important step beyond earlier theories. His attempt to link collective behavior to specific societal conditions was useful and stimulated much important research. Of special interest was his notion of structural strain, picked up by others and elaborated in important ways. Hence, Smelser's major contribution involved a demonstration of how one might approach collective behavior through an elaborate theory at several different levels of analysis. Many of the specifics were incorrect, but the general direction essentially sound. Further, his work indicated the kinds of factors one should consider in collective behavior theory. He told people where to look.

THE FRUSTRATION-AGGRESSION APPROACH TO CROWDS

Recall that Kornhauser was criticized for failing to consider specific, concrete grievances which could motivate crowd behavior. His psychological explanation of collective behavior involved a sense of "alienation" and rootlessness. In contrast, Smelser argued that crowds relflect structural strain, a perception that some situation was unacceptably inconsistent with expectations. Though an important advance, structural strain was criticized for being too general. Since virtually anything could be seen as structural strain, the concept was of limited utility. Many researchers have concurred that structural strain is too vague, and have tried to make it more specific. Probably the most interesting attempts to improve the concept involve the use of some form of the "Frustration-Aggression Hypothesis".

The Frustration-Aggression Hypothesis was originally elaborated by psychologists John Dollard and Neal E. Miller.[9] In essence, they stated that frustration leads to aggression: when situations occur which frustrate people, they become aggressive. The Frustration-Aggression Hypothesis has considerable intuitive appeal and has been applied widely in many different situations. For example, Southern lynchings were explained as a response to economic frustration. Much of the economic stability of the South rested on its cotton crop. When cotton brought a good price, people prospered. When the demand for cotton fell or when cotton was over-produced, the price of cotton dropped and economic depression resulted. Economic depression meant that white southern agricultural workers were less able to maintain a satisfactory standard of living. Hence, they became frustrated. Frustration in turn, generated aggression directed at blacks because in part blacks seemed a relatively safe and socially acceptable target .

Despite considerable plausibility, the Frustration-Aggression Hypothesis has undergone considerable criticism. One major problem is a lack of specificity for the concept of frustration. Frustration has meant all the following things at various times.

1. Frustration can mean simply the absence of certain rewards. For example, people without enough to eat might be frustrated (besides being hungry).

2. Frustration can be the absence of customary rewards. That is, people are frustrated only when they expect to be satisfied, and are not. Thus being hungry is not in itself enough to produce frustration; it is also necessary to expect to be well fed. In medieval times people survived on bread, some vegetables and occasionally a bit of meat. By modern standards, most peasants were hungry. The fact that they did not *expect* to eat any better probably minimized their frustration. Had they expected to eat as Americans today, they would have experienced considerable frustration.

3. Frustration can mean the absence of customary rewards when in addition, the obstacles to rewards are considered unreasonable. Those medieval peasants would be frustrated only when food was made scarce through factors judged capricious and illegitimate. For example, if famine occurred because of drought (about which people could do little) peasants might not feel frustrated (though still hungry). In contrast, if the lack of food resulted from an unusually greedy manor lord who exploited peasants far in excess of his feudal rights, peasants might then feel frustrated.

4. Frustration can be the result of *absolute and/or relative deprivation of rewards*. In the first case, the sense of deprivation is generated by the simple realization that one's experiences are unsatisfactory. A growling stomach might be an indicator of a lack of food. In the second case, a sense of deprivation would result from *comparing* one's current condition to some other condition among other people or at some point in time. Some Marxist scholars have argued that absolute deprivation is the key to pro-

9. John Dollard and Neal E. Miller, *Personality and Psychotherapy*, (New York: McGraw Hill, 1950).

letarian revolution. Capitalist society will reduce working people to a subsistence level and people will rebel. In contrast, other scholars (some Marxist) have argued that a low standard of living is not sufficient. Working people will feel deprived only when they compare their condition to the way rich people live or to the way they think working people should live. In practice, this difference between absolute and relative deprivation (leading to frustration) has important consequences. If absolute deprivation is the crucial factor, one would predict that societies with the poorest people would be more likely to experience aggressive behavior and hence, collective violence. If relative deprivation is the crucial factor, societies with a large gap between people's expectations and experiences will be more likely to have collective violence. Thus, relative deprivation could lead to a paradoxical situation: as objective conditions improve, the possibility of violent crowds *increases*. With a better standard of living, people begin to expect their lives to improve markedly and if the quality of life does not improve as quickly as people think it should, collective violence is likely to occur.

A second major problem with the Frustration-Aggression Hypothesis lies in the definitions of aggression. If one is trying to predict aggression, it is obviously important to specify what is meant by the term. Unfortunately "aggression" has been used in all of the following ways.

1. The *intent* to do property damage (e.g., vandalize a store).
2. The *intent* to do personal injury (e.g., lynch a rapist).
3. The *intent* to do psychological harm (e.g., to show disrespect, use sarcastic language, insult, demean).
4. Both the intent *and resulting* property damage and/or personal injury and/or psychological harm may be present. Aggression as defined here involves both the motive to aggress and the action fueled by that intent. For example, using this criteria the desire to lynch a rapist would not be sufficient for aggression. The rapist has to be lynched before "aggression" would have occurred.
5. Property damage and/or personal injury and/or psychological harm *without intent* may exist, but may occur as a byproduct of some other motive or activity. There are many different types of examples. One of the classic Orwellian tales coming out of the Vietnam war involves a statement by an American officer who ordered his men to demolish a town believed to be a communist stronghold. His explanation was that he had to "destroy the town in order to save it." "Clearly, his intent was not to destroy the town *per se*, but rather to drive away Viet Cong who were believed to be inside. Indeed, he wanted to "liberate" the area. That the town had to be destroyed was an unfortunate by-product of his desire to defeat the enemy. The theoretical question is, was the destruction of the town an instance of aggression when the real intent was to "free" it?

Given all these definitional problems, it should come as no surprise that the Frustration-Aggression Hypothesis has had a controversial history. Its application to collective behavior has produced some interesting theories and innovative empirical work. However, it is apparently far too simple to account for all collective behavior. In short, the Frustration-Aggression Hypothesis seems to account for some collective behavior some of the time.

Some of the most provocative work with the Frustration-Aggression Hypothesis has been done by political scientists. Though they typically include a rather wide range of phenomena under the heading of collective behavior (riots, rebellions, civil war, *coups d'etat,* and revolutions), we can apply their work here without serious distortions.

Most of the political science research using frustration as a cause of collective violence has defined frustration in terms of *relative deprivation.*[10] People become frustrated when their expectations about the quality of life are not met. Beginning with the work of James C. Davies, relative deprivation theory has been elaborated in several important ways to make it more applicable to the complexities of structural strain. (Actually Smelser's work and Davies' work appeared about the same time.) Davies postulated a model in which unrest was most likely to occur following a sharp decline in the quality of life, after a period of time in which both the quality of life and expectations had been rising. (See Figure 1)[11]

The graph indicates that for a period of time both "expected need satisfaction" and "actual need satisfaction" increase at parallel rates. In addition, though the expectations at any point in time are higher than actual satisfactions, the difference is not large enough to produce a sense of relative deprivation. However, if the expectations continue to rise and the ability of the society to fulfill those needs *ceases* to rise, the gap between expectations and satisfactions widens. When that gap widens abruptly, people undergo severe relative deprivation, frustration increases, and collective violence (aggression) is a likely outcome. The deprivation is called "relative" (not

"absolute") because the sense of dissatisfaction is based on past experience. In other words, people look around and notice that their lives are not improving as rapidly as they once were, or worse, their quality of life is actually deteriorating. The conditions

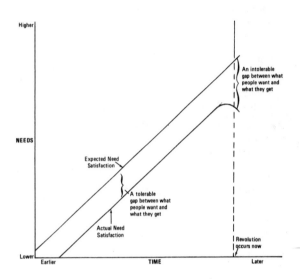

may not be bad by some absolute criteria, but bad compared to what they think they should be. Let's take the case of some underdeveloped country. Before modernization begins (the introduction of industry, formal education, health care, etc.) the standard of living may be very low, but people are used to it. They expect no better; hence they do not feel deprived. Collective violence is unlikely. Modernization begins and everyone's hopes are raised. The stan-

10. See Hugh Davis Graham and Ted Robert Gurr, ed., *The History of Violence in America,* National Commission on the Causes and Prevention of Violence, (New York: Bantam Books, 1970). Probably the most accessible source to get a feel for this work .
11. Graham and Gurr, *Violence in America,* p. **691.**

dard of living improves, people have more to eat, better medical care, and modern housing. The higher standard of living stimulates people's hope for a still better life. The quality of life keeps pace with the hopes for several years, until a severe famine cripples the economy. At that point, the hopes may still be high and rising, but the economy can no longer sustain a rising standard of living. Consequently the gap between what people expect and what occurs widens sharply. This is the period in which collective violence is most likely to appear.

Davies has produced some interesting historical data to illustrate his theory of unrest, but other researchers have found it necessary to considerably elaborate his model. Ted Gurr, Ivo K. Feierabend, and Rosalind L. Feierabend have been the most imaginative, and have developed rather complex formulations with some empirical support. Essentially, all accept the relative deprivations approach, but discuss in a *variety of ways* how a gap between expectations and satisfactions can occur. For example, the Feierabends postulate that a large gap can appear through a *rapid increase in expectation with little or no change in the standard of living.* If people's hopes are raised abruptly, even if the economy continues to operate smoothly, relative deprivation can result and collective violence becomes a likely outcome (See Figure 2).

What might cause expectations to rise so abruptly? Some people have tried to explain American Civil Disorders using just such a mechanism. In essence, they argue that black victories in the civil rights movement and a booming economy in the early sixties raised expectations sharply. In Brown vs. the Board of Education, school segregation was outlawed. Shortly afterwards, segrega-

tion in all public accommodations (e.g., restaurants, buses) was declared illegal. While legal barriers against blacks were falling, the economy was providing jobs with better pay. Finally, when President Johnson publically declared his War on Poverty, there seemed to be a national commitment to improving the lot of all poor people. For a period of time the economy continued to improve and blacks continued to make gains through congressional legislation and court victories. However, despite some real progress, the hopes of black people had escalated so rapidly that a large gap appeared between their expectations and their standard of living. This gap produced the frustration acted out in Civil Disorders. Today, the "Revolution of Rising Expectations" explanation of Civil Disorders still has some merit, but a variety of other mechanisms are needed to explain the disturbances. For example, while it is true that some legal and legislative victories were won, the standard of living for many inner city residents did not change markedly. Hence, the war on poverty may have appeared to some as a broken promise and a source of frustration.

Much of the work on the relative deprivation thesis has rested on the economic performance of a society. Unrest is said to occur when the standard of living fails to keep pace with people's expectations. As social scientists have learned more about the causes of collective violence, additional factors have been introduced. For example, even if people feel relatively deprived they will not take to the streets if that action is likely to be met with brutal repression. Therefore, countries having effective repressive regimes may prevent collective violence, even if people are prepared to revolt. In South Korea, public assembly is illegal unless sanctioned by the government. Any spontaneous demonstration is met with force, and leaders of the demonstration are often jailed and beaten. One result is that collective violence is very infrequent (though state initiated violence is common). A seminary student and South Korean describes an incident near Seoul

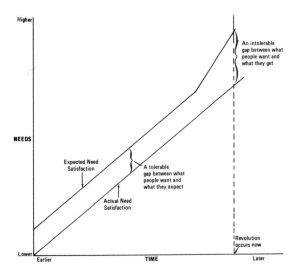

which provides an example of the ways political repression can hinder dissent. The incident developed when a community of squatters were about to be removed to make room for a housing project. No provision was made to find the squatters another place to live, and the "urban renewal" would have destroyed what little they possessed. Four men from the community had gone to see the mayor of Seoul to present the squatter's grievances. Here is an excerpt of the events in the student's own words. The English is rough, but the message will be clear.

It was originally scheduled that tearing down squatter shacks would start on March 1. Up to

February 23 the inhabitants were still calm. In the afternoon of February 24, three policemen came to the Nahk Mountain and took four young men to the police station under the condition of investigation. Many inhabitants watched the scene and they recognized the four young men were the representatives of community leaders who went to City Hall with their second petition. One old mother of the four men's was following and asking policemen to relieve them. A policeman pushed her and she fell down on the ground right beside the dangerous slope. She sat on the ground yelling out an oath to the policemen and crying for a while.

At the time, quite a number of women who watched the scene were angry and insisted to do something advocating them, because they knew what would happen to the young men. The next day all squatters found that their four young representatives could not walk out by themselves because of being beat by the policemen, and a half a dozen of their friends and families carried the four bodies on their backs out of the police station. When they came back to the Nahk Mountain slum on some friends' back all squatters who saw them wept and rather resented their poorness. It seemed that they felt not only angry but also a common fate of poverty and oppression to overcome.

Another important dimension which has been added to the relative deprivation formulation involves political rather than economic issues. Collective violence is likely to occur when certain groups are prevented from exercising their political rights. Charles Tilly argues this point in several manuscripts.

My own explorations of Western Europe, especially France, over the last few centuries suggest a more political interpretation of collective violence. Far from being mere side effects of urbanization, industrialization, and other large structural changes, violent protests seem to grow more directly from the struggle for established places in the structure of power. Even presumably nonpolitical forms of collective violence like the anti-tax revolts are normally directed against the authorities, accompanied by a critique of the authorities' failure to meet their responsibilities, and informed by a sense of justice denied to the participants in the protest. Furthermore, instead of constituting a sharp break from "normal" political life, violent protests tend to accompany, complement, and extend organized, peaceful attempts by the same people to accomplish their objectives.

Over the long run, the processes most regularly producing collective violence are those by which groups acquire or lose membership in the political community. The forms and locus of collective violence therefore very greatly depending on whether the major on-going political change is a group's acquisition of the prerequisites of membership, its loss of those prerequisites, or a shift in the organization of the entire political system.[12]

In summary, research on structural strain has come a long way in the past decade. There is wide agreement that different types of strain can facilitate collective violence. A growing body of data support various versions of the relative deprivation hypothesis, though the idea of relative deprivation is still undergoing major revisions. There are actually several different theoretical positions and new complexities are constantly being added. Obviously, much additional work needs to be done. Too often, relative deprivation is used so broadly (though far more specifically than Smelser's concept of structural strain)that its theoretical contribution is small. Further, elaborations have been attached rather unsystematically and a fundamental reconceptualization of the issues is badly needed. Currently, relative deprivation theory is simply too haphazard to be as useful as its proponents suggest.[13]

Yet Gurr, for example, claims to be able to account for many of the things that cause unrest. At this point, social scientists are vigorously addressing these issues and better data in the future should produce significant new insights.

SUMMARY AND CONCLUSIONS

Mass society explanations of collective behavior have not proven especially useful. There is little data to support a mass society perspective, and the theoretical concepts are too vague. In contrast, structural strain theory has provided many important insights. Once structural strain was elaborated through relative deprivation and other factors, societal causes of collective behavior could be more effectively labeled and investigated. When Tilly argues that relative deprivation may not be as important as orginally thought, he is not so much refuting its applicability as placing emphasis elsewhere.

These kinds of disagreements will continue in the future. The societal causes of collective behavior are extremely complex, with a variety of factors so interwined that identification of the really crucial causes will remain problematic. Nevertheless, the fact that social scientists are examining societal causes of collective behavior is by itself a vital development. An emphasis on societal causes rather than irresponsible impassioned crowd participants is an important political statement.

For Further Reading

Interesting perspectives related to the mass society literature can be found in Reissman, David. *The Lonely Crowds: A study of the Changing American Character* Rev. Ed. New Haven Conn: Yale University Press, 1950 and Slater, Phillip. *The Pursuit of Loneliness* Boston: Beacon Press, 1971. For those with a psychological bent, Fromm, Eric *Escape from*

12. Graham and Gurr, *Violence in America,* pp. 10-11.

13. There are a variety of other more subtle criticisms of a relative deprivation approach to collective behavior. They essentially boil down to the *post hoc* flavor of the perspective. Starting with a very broad conceptual base, details of the theory seem to be determined by the patterns in a particular body of data rather than by a priori mechanisms which relate logically and plausibly to one another. Instead of testing a theory with data, too much of the relative deprivation work seems based *only* on data with theory produced after the fact to account for the findings. Hopefully, relative deprivation theory will become more parsimonious in the future.

Freedom New York: Holt, Rinehart and Winston, 1941, could be useful. Finally, budding philosophers might want to take a crack at Marcuse, Herbert *An Essay of Liberation* Boston: Beacon Press, 1969 or his *One Dimensional Man* Boston: Beacon Press, 1964. However, both these works are quite difficult.

Possibly the best cross-section of work addressing various notions of structural strain can be found in Graham and Gurr cited earlier, *The History of Violence in America* New York: Bantam Books, 1970. Another excellent reader is Davies, James C. *When Men Revolt and Why,* New York: The Free Press, 1971, which presents an unusually diverse selection of material on social unrest.

There are literally hundreds of books on specific instances of unrest and social movements. If you have lots of time to do extensive reading (like over a summer), I can think of no better material than Isaac Deutcher's three volume biography of Trotsky. *The Prophet Armed,* Trotsky 1879-1921, Vol. 1, *The Prophet Unarmed,* Trotsky 1921-1929, Vol. 2, *The Prophet Outcast,* Trotsky 1929-1940, Vol. 3. All published by Vintage Press, New York. A provocative analysis of the Feminist movement can be found Firestone, Shulasmith, *The Dialectic of Sex,* New York: Bantam Books, 1971.

5 | Recent Approaches to Group Process in Collective Behavior

FROM the material discussed in Chapter 3, it is apparent that none of the traditional views on collective behavior has proven especially satisfactory. In this chapter more recent research on crowd process will be presented. Although no compelling theory of collective behavior yet exists, there is room for some optimism. Important gains have been made.

Since the unrest of the late sixties collective behavior has been a popular topic for social scientists, and many provocative studies have appeared in the literature. Most of the current work emphasizes the analysis of data on crowds. The findings are far from conclusive, but at least seriously challenge several older perspectives. Foundations of new theoretical approaches have also come to light. They are quite complicated and meld insights from psychology, sociology, and economics into an eclectic blend. Hence, in this introductory volume a somewhat superficial presentation is necessary. Nevertheless, the reader should perceive great differences between current approaches and those discussed in Chapter 3.

Probably the easiest way to introduce the material is to emphasize that many current views of collective behavior describe crowd process as *group problem solving*. The im-mediate environment and interactions between crowd participants become central concerns. The goal is to explain how people in a crowd manage to generate concerted activity with little prior preparation, under a variety of situational constraints. Before dealing with these issues in more depth, an imaginary case study should help provide a sense of these newer perspectives.

Our story opens after the first few weeks of an introductory course in sociology at a midwestern university. Fifty students are enrolled in the course, and Professor Smith has used a lecture format almost exclusively. He had promised to allot time for class discussion but had not done so after the first week or two, becoming increasingly impatient with what he thought were stupid questions.

Many of the students are sincerely interested in learning something about sociology and are prepared to be lectured at, if the material is well presented. However, by midsemester the quality of lectures begins to deteriorate. Professor Smith frequently arrives late without an apology or an excuse. More and more students realize that the lectures are not well prepared and much class time is filled with anecdotal stories having little relevance. When important issues are addressed, the presentation is disorganized.

Mary and Tom, two students in the course, soon become concerned. Both are considering majoring in sociology and realize that they are not learning much. Further, both come from homes where parents have struggled to raise tuition money. To pay a couple of thousand dollars a year for a lousy education seems unjust. They decide to talk to the teacher about the course.

For two weeks Mary and Tom try to meet with Professor Smith. Twice, immediately after class they attempt to strike up a conversation, but Smith always seems to be in a hurry to go somewhere. He curtly answers their questions about class material, but is unapproachable on any other topic. Finally, Mary and Tom decide to make an appointment to see Smith after class. They ask the departmental secretary when they might see the professor only to find that he has cancelled his office hours and generally leaves the campus soon after his teaching is completed. One day after class Tom and Mary ask Smith directly for a short conference, but the professor says he's too busy.

Weeks pass and the situation does not improve. The lectures get more and more boring and less relevant. Large numbers of students are cutting and those who come to class spend most of the time daydreaming. No one asks questions and Smith does not seem to care.

With one week left in the semester, Smith announces that the final exam will be in an essay format. Students will be given two hours to write on four questions. Eight questions will be given and each student can pick the four he/she prefers. Students find this procedure fair and are especially pleased when Smith describes in detail the material to be covered on the exam.

Exam day arrives and things don't go as expected. While passing out the exam, Smith indicates that its format is multiple choice. He explains that he does not have the time to grade fifty essay exams, and in any case, a multiple choice test will better separate the wheat from the chaff.

After all the exams are passed out, Smith sits down at his desk in the front of the room. He explains that he is going to look over the exam for typographical errors, then go back to his office to grade papers from another course. He plans to check back with the class from time to time and will pick up all exams in two hours.

As the students begin to work on the exam, they notice that some of the material was not covered in class and is not about the topics the professor said would be included. Many of the students who were already anxious about the course now begin to feel they will not pass the exam. Even the conscientious students are worried.

After about fifteen minutes Smith gets up to leave saying that he will check back with them. As soon as he leaves grumbling begins. Students know they are not supposed to talk during exams, yet several students begin complaining to one another in whispers. One student snaps his pencil in two, another rolls some paper into a ball and throws it against a window and another mutters loudly "Oh shit." The comment draws a few nervous laughs. About five minutes pass with students trying to work on the exam. The grumbling continues. Then one student, Bill gets up and walks to the front of the room where unused exams are stacked on Smith's desk. His hunch is correct; among the papers is an exam with all the answers marked. With the discovery in hand he announces, "Guess what folks, here are the answers."

Everyone had watched Bill thumbing through the stack of exams, but were a bit surprised at the consequences. A couple of people even felt they should have told him to sit down when he started toward the front of the room, but now aren't so sure. On one hand, using the answers would obviously be cheating. Further, if everyone used the answers, Smith would probably suspect the truth. Finally, even if he did not become suspicious, everyone would do well, rewarding students who had not worked in the course. On the other hand, good and poor students alike are baffled by the exam. Much of the material seems new and many of the question ambiguous. Further, students resent the way the course had been run.

Mary stands up, "Why don't we all share the answers. If everyone purposely misses a few items, the professor will not catch on."

Students begin talking to one another, some agree with Mary's proposal, others are against it. In one corner, Pete and Sam and Sally are arguing among themselves about the ethics of cheating. In the middle of the room Jane, Bob, and Don are more concerned with how to make it look like they had not used the answers. In general most of the students are ambivalent, torn between wishing to cheat and its negative implications.

Emily then speaks up, "While you are talking about the answers, time is flying. We have already wasted 5 minutes and this is a long exam. Let's get back to work."

Pat responds, "Look, Professor Smith will be back any minute. If he walks in on us now, we'll be in trouble."

Bill answers, "Don't panic, he won't be back for a half hour. He is grading exams and has other things on his mind."

At that point Mary speaks up again. "I heard that Professor Smith gave a real tough exam last year, but graded on a curve so it does not matter if we all do poorly. He grades on a heavy B curve."

By now everyone in the room is talking. Some are trying to figure out when Smith is likely to return. Some are comparing information about what they had heard about Smith's grading policy. Some wanted to get on with the exam and are grumbling that time is being wasted. As time passes the conversations get louder and louder. Some decision has to be made, and soon.

After five more minutes, Bill, who has returned to his seat suggests, "Look, we don't have to make up our minds now. Why don't we wait for Smith to return? After he leaves again we can share the answers. If everyone purposely misses a few he will not catch on and if he does, he will not be able to pin the blame on anyone. He's been irresponsible with us, I don't see any reason why we should flunk on account of him."

Pete speaks up, "I agree that Smith has been unfair, but two wrongs don't make a right."

Jane, who is feeling more and more flustered, responds, "We don't have time for a fancy debate about moral issues. The point is either we all cooperate or we might as well get back to the the exam."

Finally Mary proposes, "How about this? Those who want to use the answers can. Those who don't want to don't have to. All that is necessary is that those who don't use the answers don't tell on those who do use them. OK?"

There is a flurry of animated conversation; people are really getting edgy. Time is passing, Smith may return at any moment, and there is still the exam to be done.

Emily gains the attention of the class and announces, "I don't want to be any part of this. We all could be thrown out of school."

By this time Mary is quite angry, "Look Emily, you've got a simple choice. We're going to use the answers. If you do not want to use them, fine. But if you turn us in you'll get us all canned. No one is forcing you to cheat. Just don't side with Smith. If you get us thrown out of school, the word will get out that you turned us in, and no one will ever have anything to do with you on this campus again."

At this point many people in the class respond. "Yeah, that's right. . . ." "Look Emily, just mind your own business. . . ." "Emily go stick your head in an oven. . . ."

Some students are sympathetic with Emily's position, but statements against her draw such widespread support that no one else speaks on her behalf.

Bill senses that the class is about ready to cooperate and says, "OK, are there any other objections?" A pause. "Fine, after Smith comes back and leaves again, we'll pass around the answers. Those who don't want to use them just pass them along. But we all keep quite about this, right?"

People in the class nod and a few give verbal assent. Then they sit quietly in their seats waiting for Smith to return. About five minutes later Smith walks in and asks if there are any questions. When no one answers, he says he will stop back in later and leaves the room. Immediately, Mary goes to the desk, takes the answers and begins passing them out.

(The student should pause now and try to put himself/herself in the shoes of the people in Smith's class. How would you have felt? What would you have done? What do you think was going on?)

What can one abstract from these events? Let's work inductively and see what emerges.

1. Prior to the exam, Professor Smith had been unsatisfactory as a teacher. Students had certain expectations about their introductory course which Smith failed to meet. Those expectations were grounded in basic ideas about the educational process and

what tuition money should buy. Hence, students were experiencing *relative deprivation.*

2. Two students, at least, tried to talk to Smith about the course, but he did not cooperate. *Channels for communication* were largely absent, and even if students had been able to express their grievances, it is unlikely Smith would have responded favorably.

3. Before the day of the exam, there were no plans to cheat. Students had not considered what they would do should exam answers be available. They probably thought about many of the issues before, and may even have cheated in the past, but one could not say their behavior during the exam was planned in advance. Rather the behavior could be characterized as *spontaneous.*

4. The exam was the last in a series of events which students felt violated their sense of fair play. It focused attention on grievances about the course and reminded everyone about their experience during the semester. Hence, the exam acted as a *precipitating incident* by drawing people to a given location and creating the potential for group action.

5. When Smith left the room and Bill found the answers to the exam, the students were presented with an *opportunity.* Built into the situation were a number of potential *benefits* and a number of potential *costs.* For example, cheating successfully might bring benefits, but the moral implications and the possibility of getting caught might bring costs.

6. Students had a *variety of reactions* to the opportunity. Some wanted to cheat, others did not. Most were unsure of what actions should be taken: they felt ambivalent. There was no evidence of a "generalized belief" that is, a common, dominant perception of the situation that was naive, magical, or a "short-circuit" of reality. Rather, students considered a variety of factors such as how much they valued various outcomes (like getting an "A" through cheating) and the chances that certain kinds of events might occur (like the chance Smith would return in the middle of their discussion).

7. Many of the students were *highly motivated.* First, all were anxious about the exam and most resented the course and the multiple choice exam format. Second, the consequences of their action could have important effects on their lives. Third, as the discussion continued there was additional reason for worry. Time was being used that could have been applied to the exam, and Smith could return at any moment. There was, therefore, the chance they might be "busted" for a discussion of cheating even if cheating had not actually occurred. Finally, the discussion itself produced anxiety. Pressure was being applied to many students with threats of retaliation for unacceptable behavior. Some students were put in a bind of choosing between their friends and their conscience. Some students had to choose between their friends and a concern that their entire class would be caught cheating.[1]

1. When psychologists speak of "motivation" the term is usually applied broadly to include the seeking of positive (desirable) outcomes, the avoidance of negative (undesirable) outcomes, and in the case of clinical psychologists, a sense of fear without a specific conscious cause. For example, hunger is a positive motivation, pain is a negative motivation and anxiety is an ill defined sense of distress with no specific referent. Many psychologists argue that motives can be additive in their impact. That is, a person who is moderately hungry and moderately anxious is not moderately motivated, but highly motivated because the effects of the two motives combine. In the cheating example, students had many motives which added together to produce an overall high level of motivation.

8. The students were faced with many ambiguities and unknowns. Would Smith grade on a curve? What were the chances of getting caught? Would the class stick together? When might Smith return? Therefore, in their desire to make the most sensible choice, substantial energies were directed towards assessing the situation. The process by which people informally gather and collectively evaluate information is called *rumor;* and one could consider the discussion about Smith's B curve a rumor introduced to aid in decision-making. If Smith would actually grade generously, cheating would be less desirable.

9. Though interaction in the classroom was *face-to-face,* there was no indication of "contagion" or "suggestion," or "circular reaction." Rather, each person tried to *assess the situation,* decide the *best outcomes,* and then *persuade others to go along.*

10. A crucial factor for each student was the likelihood that they would all stick together. The entire plan would disintegrate unless students *supported each other.* Everyone did not have to cheat, but no one could be permitted to reveal that cheating had occurred. In short, everyone had to consider what others were likely to do before deciding whether to cheat. Their fates were thoroughly entwined.

11. While consensus was being hammered out, a set of informal rules (or norms) to govern the consensus were also emerging. In other words, the group decisions carried a set of explicit and implied definitions of the situation (e.g., It's OK to cheat since Smith has been unjust). and norms regulating behavior. Backing the norms were a set of sanctions. For example, it was OK not to cheat, but anyone who squealed would be ostracized.

12. Though some students led the discussion more than others, there was no evidence of *one* demagogic leader appealing to base, unconscious impulses. "Leaders" acted more as discussion directors; making suggestions, providing information, focusing attention on specific topics, and fostering decision-making.

13. Finally, the actions in the classroom were limited to that setting. Though conceivably an ongoing student group to improve teaching at the university could have emerged, as the incident was described, the activity was *transitory.* No one proposed forming a student committee to pressure for Smith's dismissal.

In summary, one could call the incident an instance of collective behavior. The availability of exam answers provided an opportunity to remedy grievances, and *consensual* support for cheating was the crucial element for *group* action. Each individual had to consider his/her own interests and then be prepared to *negotiate* with others in order to arrive at a *consensus.* The classroom incident is analagous to the actions of a parliament or legislature where members try to advance their interests through compromise. The main differences between a legislature and our cheating incident are (a) the legislative decision-making is more structured through rules of parliamentary procedure, (b) the legislature will persist through time facilitating the development of informal rules for behavior (e.g., freshman legislators should not introduce important bills), and (c) there are more formal mechanisms in legislatures to hold members accountable for their actions (e.g., elections). However, even these are differences of degree, not kind. First, all legislators know that the formal rules have loopholes which allow a variety of spontaneous actions to occur. Second, over time a cohort of students builds up many informal understandings which provide structure; the cheating students had had a semester to get acquainted, had taken exams before and knew what was expected, and could anticipate contact with one another in the future. They too had informal rules for behavior. Finally, should the student actions be revealed, there were formal mechanisms to hold them accountable. (It would be useful at this point to reread the description of the incident in Congress from Chapter 1.)

With the above material as a background, a more formal presentation of some important theoretical trends can be presented. Throughout, reference will be made to the three collective behavior incidents described in Chapter 1.

DECISION THEORY

People have always sought ways of making good decisions; and sages, scholars, politicians and businessmen have provided a variety of suggestions. Some advice has come in the form of folk wisdom: "When you are angry count to ten before doing anything." Or, "Before buying a used car, kick the tires." Some of the advice has been formulated in more complicated ways: novels, poems, political analyses, and philosophy.

Over the past twenty years scholars have increasingly employed mathematics to advise people how to make good decisions. Some of the formulations are very complex and though mathematically valid, have little use in actual problems. However, the body of knowledge under the heading of "Decision Theory" appears to be a useful mix of mathematical tools and consideration for real constraints. In essence, Decision Theory suggests how people should assess their environments before making a decision. Raiffa, one of the leading proponents of Decision Theory suggests,

1) list the viable options available to you for gathering information, for experimentation, and for action;
2) list the events that may possibly occur;
3) arrange in chronological order the information you may acquire and the choices you make as time goes on;
4) decide how well you like the consequences that result from the various course of actions open to you; and
5) judge what the chances are that any particular uncertain event will occur.[2]

All that Raiffa is really saying is find out how to get as much information as possible about the situation, try to figure out what is likely to occur, list the options for action you have, rank the results of your action in terms of desired results, and then select the course of action that brings you the most satisfactory results.

Raiffa's five steps can be mathematized, and in that form are a *prescriptive* strategy for decision-making. That is, the formulation tells a person how to act in order to maximize the chances of getting a desired result. It can also be applied as a gauge of real events that have already occurred, to determine if the actors employed decision-making processes like Raiffa suggests. If one defines rationality in Raiffa's terms, as a *process* through which sound decisions can be made, it becomes possible to assess how "rationally" people in crowds (and people more generally) behave.

Think back to the imaginary classroom example. There was evidence of people seeking information, trying to assess the chance certain events would occur (like whether Smith would return), listing options for action (to cheat or not), attaching preferences to various outcomes (getting caught would be bad), and then attempting

2. Howard Raiffa, *Decision Analysis*, (Reading, Mass: Addison Wesley, 1970,) p. 10.

to make decisions which would provide the best result.

Similar processes were at work in the barricade construction example. Students sought information, tried to determine what might happen (like whether they would be busted), listed options (build a barricade, go back to the dormitory, etc.), ranked various outcomes (getting busted would be bad), and attempted to produce the best outcome.

One can postulate similar processes in the minds of many of the soldiers at My Lai when the incident is examined in detail. During the weeks preceding the massacre, Charlie Company had experienced a variety of frustrations. Though "psyched up" for combat, they had little contact with Viet Cong. Nevertheless, they were harassed with sniper fire from time to time and lost several men in booby traps. Morale was low as the company's patrols seemed unable to generate a "showdown" with large numbers of the enemy. Rather, they were spending most of their time marching through hot jungle in seemingly purposeless activity. As time passed, more and more of the troops began to kill civilians and mistreat prisoners. Shortly before being ordered to "take" My Lai, one of the most popular soldiers was killed by a land mine. At his burial Captain Medina, the officer in charge, made a short speech exorting his men to be aggressive in the next day's mission. One soldier recalls Medina saying that "nothing would be walking, growing, or crawling after Charlie Company was through." Hence, the men who entered My Lai had a variety of hostile motives. All hoped to kill Viet Cong, many were ready to kill anything.

It is not clear to this day whether Captain Medina ordered the massacre of civilians. Calley apparently did order some soldiers to shoot men, women, and children. Now, consider the kind of decision each soldier had to make. If he wanted to kill civilians he had to first decide what the consequences of that action might involve. Would he be given a medal, court martialed, or be pretty much ignored? Would Calley or Medina see him shoot civilians, and if so, what would they say? Had Medina ordered (or at least condoned) a massacre? Also, each soldier had to consider how he felt about killing innocent people. For example, "Roy Wood, one of Calley's men who was working next to Brooks' platoon, stormed into a hut, saw an elderly man hiding inside along with his wife and two daughters: 'I hit him with my rifle and pushed him out.' A GI from Brooks' platoon, standing by with an M79 grenade launcher, asked to borrow his gun. Wood refused, and the soldier asked another platoon mate. He got the weapon, said, 'Don't let none of them live,' and shot the Vietnamese in the head."[3] Though this data is too incomplete to make a good case, there were clearly differences of opinion about killing civilians. One way these differences could have appeared is through different individual assessments of the situation. The point is that each soldier weighed a variety of factors before deciding to shoot civilians.

Finally, there is the example taken from Congressional price control debate. There is no need to examine it again in detail. The reporter describes how Congressmen arrived at decisions through processes much like Raiffa would require for "rationality."

In summary, Decision Theory may provide a better foundation for the examination of crowd processes than do earlier perspectives. By emphasizing rational thought

3. Hersh, *My Lai*, page 52.

processes it becomes possible to account for a variety of phenomena inexplicable through earlier approaches. For example, "circular reaction" cannot account for the fact that real dialogue, not just herd-like stimulation, occurs during the generation of collective behavior. There were legitimate exchanges of ideas in all the examples presented. However, one important caveat should be emphasized, Decision Theory *would not rule out* unconscious motives for behavior. Rather, Decision Theory implies (a) that unconscious motivation may be less important for collective behavior than originally supposed, (b) that unconscious motivation is at least no more important in crowds than elsewhere, and (c) that collective behavior should not be defined, as theorists like Smelser did, through alleged inferior mental processes of crowd members. One final example may help make the point that people can approximate Raiffa's criteria under stress and when decisions must be made in a hurry.

The Baltimore Colts and Chicago Bears are engaged in a tie game with time running out in the fourth quarter of the Super Bowl XII. The Bears are on the Colt's 35 yardline and the Bear's quarterback has called an intricate crossing pattern involving the tight end and flanker back. As he approaches the line of scrimmage he notices that the Colts are in a zone defense which will likely rotate towards his primary and secondary receivers. Immediately he calls an audible and his wide receiver becomes the primary target with the fullback as an emergency outlet. The ball is snapped, the quarterback backpeddles and sees that his wide receiver is covered. He looks to the fullback but he has been knocked down by an aggressive linebacker. As his pass protection starts to break down the quarterback tries to find another open receiver. While ducking under a charge of a defensive end who has broken through the pocket, the quarterback notices that the middle linebacker has dropped back for pass coverage and the middle of the Colt defense is vulnerable. He tucks the ball, and scrambles up the middle. Fifteen yards down field he picks up a block from his tight end, breaks a tackle of the safety and runs into the end zone. The Bears win and Mayor Daley gives the Bear quarterback a key to the city and a patronage job for his retirement.

Think back over this example. Every player on the field had to make a variety of split-second decisions, especially the quarterback who had to alter his plans continually. He was able to change his play, and then invent a new strategy when that play failed. During this time, about ten seconds, he had to assess all kinds of complicated information while under tremendous stress and intense motivation. Obviously, people are able to make very difficult decisions under very trying circumstances. People in crowds are no exception. *Unless one is prepared to admit that crowd participants can assess their environments in a manner roughly like Raiffa describes, linking the behavior of crowds to their complex and constantly changing environment becomes extremely problematic.* During civil disorders, stores owned by blacks were less likely to be vandalized than stores owned by whites. Obviously some black rioters were selecting their targets. The most plausible explanation is that rational decision-making was occurring within the collective behavior.

THE ROLE OF RUMOR

Among the earliest subjects attacked by empirical American social science was the nature of rumor. The "classic" studies evolved from interest in the ways errors appeared during the informal transmission of information. Rumors were characterized as oral communication among people which resulted in distortions and falsification of information. Rumors could occur in almost any setting and describe almost any subject. For example, in virtually every war movie, the GI's talk about the "scuttlebutt from up top," where their company will be stationed next, the chance of getting "liberty," or who is "in dutch" with the "Old Man."

Until rather recently, the most influential work on rumor was produced by Allport and Postman. Using laboratory experiments on human subjects, they sought to simulate rumor process under easily observable conditions. One person was shown an ambiguous picture of some human interaction. For example, a black person might be sitting next to a white person in a bus with the white person looking out the window and the black person looking straight ahead. The subject was then asked to tell some other person what the picture was about. This second subject then told a third and so on. Each communication could be heard only by the two interacting people and the researchers. At each step in the chain of communication the content of the message was recorded, and from this data, Postman and Allport were able to document how the story was changed from each telling.

For many years the Allport-Postman findings were among the "basic truths" uncovered by social scientists. Shibutani describes their conclusions as follows. "They summarize their findings in terms of three concepts: *levelling* designates the tendency of accounts to become shorter, more concise, and more easily grasped; *sharpening*, the tendency towards selective perception,

retention, and reporting of a limited number of details; and *assimilation*, the tendency of reports to become more coherent and more consistent with the presuppositions and interests of the subjects."[4] In the example of the picture of the white and black men sitting on the bus, the message might eventually be that the black man was glaring at the white man. Other details are lost and the black-white tension is emphasized.

More recently, the general applicability of the Allport-Postman laboratory studies has been widely challenged. Though there are many technical criticisms, they essentially boil down to the artificiality of a laboratory setting. Data gathered from actual instances of rumor in natural settings suggest that rumors are not necessarily distortions and in fact, may provide crucial and accurate assessments. To quote Shibutani, ". . . rumor will be regarded as recurrent form of communication through which men caught together in an ambiguous situation attempt to construct a meaningful interpretation of it by pooling their intellectual resources. It might be regarded as a form of collective problem-solving."[5] In other words, a rumor is an attempt of a group of people to understand their situation. In the cheating example, students were trying to decide whether cheating would be a productive action. The information that Professor Smith might grade on a B curve is an instance of rumor, an attempt to make sense of the situation.

Shibutani also argues that people often play a variety of roles in the production of rumor. "The contribution made by each person varies with the character of his involve-

4. Tamotsu Shibutani, *Improvised News,* Bobbs-Merrill, New York, 1966, p. 5.
5. Shibutani, *Improvised News,* p. 17.

ment in the situation and his relationship to the others. Participants in rumor construction enact various roles. Most obvious is the role of *messenger*, the person who brings a pertinent item of information to the group. He usually sees himself as relaying something he has heard, even though he is reporting the information from an idiosyncratic standpoint. Another common role is that of *interpreter*, the person who tries to place the news in context, evaluating it in the light of past events and speculating on the implications for the future. The *skeptic* is the one who expresses doubt over the authenticity of the report, demands proof, and urges caution about using it as a basis for adjustment. When there are several possible interpretations or plans of action, the *protagonist* sponsors one over the others. Sometimes he is an individual who is personally affected, such as a relative or close friend of someone who has been victimized; if so, he may become an *agitator*. In rare instances a person who believes a report to be false may support it to encourage beliefs that serve his interests. The most frequently assumed role is that of *auditor*, often a spectator who says very little. Those who indicate their interests and merely listen, only occasionally raising a question, are nonetheless important, for their very presence affects the developing outlook. What each speaker says is organized in a manner designed to appeal to his listeners, and the attitudes imputed to those who pay attention affect communication content. A key role is that of the *decision-maker*, who takes the lead in determining what ought to be done."[6]

Rumors can develop in a variety of situations. When applied to crowds, rumor is simply an attempt by group members to generate information which will facilitate decision-making. Characteristically, the de-

sired information is not readily available through formal channels and the information must come from the limited resources that crowd members have on hand.

Shibutani distinguishes two key types of situations which affect the process by which rumors are produced. First, when crowd members have considerable time, when the demand for information is not too intense, and when "collective excitement is mild," rumor construction occurs through "*critical deliberation.*" In other words, if people can calmly consider their situation, the processes will be orderly and reasoned. Further, rumors produced under such favorable circumstances have a greater chance of being accurate assessments.

The second type of rumor formation occurs under the conditions of Blumer's "circular reaction." When the demand for information is very great, and "collective excitement" is intense, Shibutani calls the rumor process "*extemporaneous.*" Note, he is not saying that various external pressures like an absence of time or poor communication undermine a rumor's accuracy. Shibutani is arguing that the *mental capabilities* of crowd members are altered so that they become less rational and less able to critically consider their situation. In short, we are returned once again to the spectre of the irrational crowd.

In summary, research on rumor provides important insights into the ways crowds construct consensual interpretations of their environments. Recent views that rumors are not necessarily inaccurate fit nicely into the Decision Theory framework discussed earlier. Once we disregard the view that rumors in crowds are necessarily produced by people whose critical abilities are inopera-

6. Shibutani, *Improvised News,* p. 17.

tive, much of the recent work on rumor becomes extremely useful. Note, this is not to say that people always weigh the facts carefully. Rather, an inability to exercise rational thought is *not* a function of crowd participation. A person sitting alone on his/her front porch might be less perceptive about a given situation than an "excited" crowd member.

Of special import in the future may be Shibutani's description of the variety of roles people play in rumor formation. This division of labor applied to crowds is yet another blow against theoretical perspectives which emphasize crowd homogeneity, and reflects the kind of interpersonal complexity that must be unraveled. (It is worth mentioning in passing that Shibutani surprisingly saw no inconsistency between complex division of labor in rumor formation and his application of Blumer's "circular reaction"!)

COLLECTIVE DECISION-MAKING AND EMERGENT NORMS

Our discussion of rumor leads directly into the work of Ralph H. Turner and Lewis M. Killian. For Turner and Killian the key issue in collective behavior is "not to explain" why an unnatural unanimity develops," but to explain "the imposition of patterns of differential expression which is perceived as unanimity by crowd members. . ."[7] In other words, people in crowds don't all behave alike, yet their actions are perceived by participants as reflecting an important consensus. This apparent paradox is explained through the concept of an "emergent norm." Crowd members may be behaving in somewhat different ways, but all behavior is consistent with a common set of goals and is governed by shared, informal rules generated by the crowd. When the barricade was built on Sheridan Road,

Turner and Killian would argue that a range of behavior occurred. Some people gathered material for the barricade, some helped move the fence to the appropriate intersection, some stood around lending verbal encouragement. Yet all actions had the same ultimate effect (to help build a barricade), and crowd members knew what kinds of actions were consistent with that goal and which were not. The norms (shared, informal rules governing the behavior) are called *emergent* because they are quite specific to the situation and are produced largely for that occasion. Hence, Emergent Norm approaches to collective behavior are really explanations of the ways norms evolve and how behavioral conformity with the norms occurs. Two conformity producing mechanisms are implied by the Turner-Killian approach. First, deviant behavior (i.e., behavior inconsistent with the emergent norms) is likely to be explicitly punished and conformity explicitly rewarded. Think back to the classroom example. Second, people tend to conform to norms unconsciously. While the psycho-dynamics of this process are not well understood, the psychological concept of "secondary reinforcement" seems especially relevant. In essence, if a particular action is frequently rewarded (e.g., praise for cleanliness) that action soon becomes rewarding *in itself*. The primary reinforcement (praise) is no longer necessary to sustain the behavior, the behavior *per se* (cleanliness) provides its own reward.[8] People simply learn to prefer

7. Ralph H. Turner and Lewis M. Killian, Collective Behavior, 2nd ed., © 1972, p. 80. By permission of Prentice-Hall, Inc., Englewood Cliffs, New Jersey.

8. Technically, "primary reinforcement "refers only to the basic physical rewards (food, water, sex, etc.). While "secondary reinforcement" refers to all other rewards which are not biological but learned.

cleanliness and typically cease to question its validity. In the case of crowds, since conformity is likely to have been highly rewarded in the past in a variety of contexts (not just in crowds, in everyday life), conformity becomes its own unquestioned reward. Therefore, people are apt to "habitually" conform both in their perceptions of a situation and in their behavior. Further, if such an insight is indeed relevant for crowds, it is important to emphasize that this mechanism (habitual conformity) rather than explicit reward and punishment, is far more salient in the Turner-Killian perspective. *People conform to emergent norms primarily because unconsciously they are prepared to follow the dictates of the group (or crowd).*

It is important to emphasize the continuity between this Emergent Norm approach to crowds and the kinds of comformity that occur daily. You go to a movie and talk too loudly with a friend. What happens? Usually people tell you to shut up. You wear shirts with button down collars when they are "out." What happens? Someone asks if you got those shirts from your grandfather. A guy trying out for his high school football team ducks his head while trying to tackle. What happens? The Coach tells him to join the Pom Pom girls. Clearly, pressures supplementing habitual conformity are a daily experience. Conformity in crowds differ in degree: the standards to which people are supposed to conform are meant to apply primarily to the situation in which crowd members find themselves. At My Lai, the emergent norms encouraging wholesale killing of civilians were not just limited to Vietnam, but to the specific My Lai mission.

There is an important implication of this continuity between conformity in crowds and more general conformity: emergent norms may evolve when people are highly aroused or when they are placid. There is no need to postulate a heightened emotionality to explain crowd behavior. Hence, Emergent Norm approaches break significantly with earlier contagion theories which emphasized emotional arousal and impulsiveness. However, Turner and Killian *do* argue that crowd members are *less* able than people in other contexts to rationally consider their environments. The mechanism is not circular reaction or some other condition stimulating powerful impulses. Rather, crowd members are less able to carefully consider their actions because the pressure toward conformity excludes an especially wide range of issues which are inconsistent with the emergent norms. "Thus on the group level there is the emergence of a norm. On the individual level there is heightened suggestibility but this suggestibility is not of an unfocused indiscriminate nature. It amounts to a tendency to respond uncritically to suggestions that are consistent with the mood, imagery, and conception of appropriate action that have developed and assume a normative character.[9] For example, at My Lai one of the norms condoning the slaughter was the common view among Charlie Company (and American soldiers in general) that Vietnamese were somehow subhuman; they considered all *Vietnamese* "gooks." As Charlie Company entered My Lai this norm became especially salient (possibly as a justification for expressing a more general resentment). At this point, a variety of considerations inconsistent with this view were less likely to be weighed. If the villagers were "gooks," it was not necessary to judge

9. Turner and Killan, *Collective Behavior,* p. 80.

actions in terms of the murder of human beings. Hence, the GIs' were responding "uncritically" to the situation.

One can postulate emergent norm effects in the Congressional example as well. During the committee session in which the price "roll back" bill was discussed "some committee members started competing to see who could sound and act the toughest in going after the "price gougers." With the situation defined in normative terms as an opportunity to play to local voters, many other considerations (e.g., would the bill have a good chance of passage) were ignored. Norms encouraging the competition and public relations rhetoric greatly restricted the number of factors the congress weighed.

Turner and Killian see a prominent place for rumor in their formulation. Using an approach very much like Shibutani's, they argue that rumors are part of a process aiding in the evolution of emergent norms. When "traditional understandings" fail to supply the means for assessing a situation, or when institutional and habitual arrangements do not adequately aid in the coordination of a group of individuals, rumors provide definitions and suggest appropriate collective activity. In other words, rumors aid groups in organizing appropriate action when people initially fail to understand what's going on and don't know what to do. When Professor Smith's students were trying to organize themselves, the rumor about Smith's B curve provided an important definition of the situation and suggested appropriate action.

In summary, an emergent norm approach to crowds (in which conformity to situationally specific norms becomes the central explanatory mechanism) identifies factors largely ignored by earlier theorists. There is good evidence that people in crowds, like people in any group, respond to the expectations of their peers. Unfortunately, although quite useful, Emergent Norm perspectives are still at best incomplete.

1. There are few theoretical concepts which attempt to formally link the development of specific norms to their causes. While several group processes are suggested as explanatory mechanisms (e.g. "keynoting" in which leaders focus attention on particular issues), these mechanisms are extremely limited in ability to unravel crowd behavior. Indeed, it is almost as if norms evolve from thin air, or more fairly, from broad ambiguities in a situation. In My Lai for example, an emergent norm analysis would indicate a role for Captain Medina's ambiguous orders, but could not provide a detailed explanation of how and why slaughtering civilians was the *particular* norm that became operative. Why did the soldiers not choose to kill only men instead, or only men of military age, or only men who resisted? Why was killing the mode of action? Beating civilians could have served many of the same functions. In the congressional example, why did the norm of competition develop? Though one might propose a variety of *post hoc* explanations, emergent norm approaches define few concepts which specify the relevant factors, let alone explain their effects. The fact that norms can be found operating is clearly an important insight, but unless one can indicate in some detail where the norms come from and by what mechanisms, it is impossible to understand the actions of crowds.

2. Related to the first criticism is the theory's failure to specifically examine the environments in which crowds operate. Since the evolution of norms requires contact and communication between crowd

participants, one should expect that the environments in which these interactions occur would be of some relevance. Does it matter if a crowd is arranged in a dense circle or strung out over several city blocks? If a crowd weaves around several corners (like during a march) people will be unable to hear and see events around the next bend and communication will be hindered. If the crowd is very dense, people will only be able to see events near by. Important actions and statements from other members will be missed. Does it matter if it's daylight and people can see one another? At night with visual contact limited, communication is likely to be severely altered. And so on. The important point is that an emergent norm approach treats crowds almost as if they existed on a "featureless plain," or are somehow anesthetized to the details of their surroundings.

3. Also related to the first criticism is a failure to address in detail the nature of the interactions between *individual* crowd members. Turner and Killian note that people come to crowds somewhat confused but with a variety of possible interpretations of the situation and ideas for action. What happens to these individuals? How do they interact with one another? In the example from the Sheridan Road barricade, some students wanted to go back to the dormitory, some wanted to stage a sit down, some wanted to "trash" downtown stores, and some wanted to build a barricade. This complexity at the individual unit of analysis seems lost through emergent norm views. While norms are evolving, the role of specific crowd members in that process is not considered. Only broad group dynamics are addressed.

4. Turner and Killian never provide a convincing explanation of why crowd mem-

bers are *less* able to critically examine their situation than people in other circumstances. They seem to *assume* crippled cognitive abilities. While the first three criticisms above reflect the incomplete nature of Emergent Norm theory, here it seems that Turner and Killian may simply be wrong.

In conclusion, Emergent Norm approaches need considerable elaboration. By emphasizing group pressures in the production of conformity in crowds, one can get the misleading impression that there is no external reality to be carefully considered. By focusing on *group* pressure, the actions of specific individuals are largely ignored. Finally, the case that crowd members are especially irrational is not made.

GAMING APPROACHES TO CROWDS

Gaming approaches to crowds try to delineate the theoretical mechanisms through which crowds respond to their environments and to each other. Resting heavily on Decision Theory, the gathering of a crowd is viewed as an *opportunity* in which individuals can experience certain rewards and certain costs. Each individual tries to maximize rewards and minimize costs. Recall that Decision Theory emphasized the following notions.

While trying to minimize costs and maximize rewards (loosely called a "minimax" strategy), each individual considers several different issues. First, a person figures out how to gather information about the situation. In the case of My Lai, one of the most important concerns for each soldier was to discover ways of finding out whether an order to kill civilians had really been given. Who should he talk to; who would know if the order had been given? Second, a person lists events that might occur. At My Lai "events" would include an order to shoot civilians, resistance from civilians, and finding only women and children in the village. Third, a person arranges the events according to the time sequence in which they might occur and decides where options for action might be available along the way. For example, a member of Calley's platoon might weigh the following. "If Calley orders me to shoot civilians, I have two options: shoot civilians or try to talk him out of it. If I decide to shoot civilians, that's the end of it. If I try to talk Calley out of it and he changes his mind, that's the end of it. If I try to talk him out of it and fail, I have two more choices: shoot civilians or refuse to obey the order."[10] Fourth, a person decides how well he/she likes the outcomes of the various possible actions. Our soldier at My Lai might wish neither to shoot civilians nor to disobey an order, but prefer to shoot civilians as the lesser of two costs. Fifth, a person determines the likelihood that various events might occur. For example, a soldier at My Lai might figure the odds at about fifty-fifty that a direct order to shoot civilians would be given. Or the odds might be about twenty-five-seventy-five that Calley would rescind the order. Finally, given a series of expectations about what events are likely to occur, a person chooses actions with "minimax" outcomes. If shooting civilians is the least of alternative evils, that should be the action undertaken. (This example is not meant to imply that the presence of absence of Calley's orders was the only or even primary factor at My Lai.)

It was argued earlier that the six steps just reviewed can be a useful gauge of the mental processes of individual crowd members. If this is a plausible supposition, then Decision Theory provides the theoretical tools which link crowd members to each other and to their environment. The environment is a source of information about a variety of events and payoffs. Each crowd member tries to act in ways which generate the best outcome for himself/herself in light of the environment. In the My Lai example, the shooting of civilians was not just a function of some emergent norm encouraging the slaughter, but of the fact that "real" Vietcong were not present, that the men were not closely supervised by Medina, that the people put up no resistance, and a host of other situational factors to which each soldier reacted.

When Decision Theory is applied to crowds, one situational factor receives special attention because it is a key element transforming an aggregate of people into a crowd. Each crowd member must consider *what other people in the crowd are likely to do*. Would you have started to build a barricade on Sheridan Road if everyone else was going to simply walk up the street leaving you alone? Would you have decided to cheat on Professor Smith's exam if you knew others might report you? Would you stand up in a congressional committee and give a slam-bang emotional oration if others were interested in a quiet consideration of the facts? Would you have shot civilians,

10. A person would not typically verbalize these assessments in order to perform them. Recall the Chicago Bear quarterback. He made many complex judgments in several seconds without the use of language. Or, consider a common situation where you are driving a car on a two-lane highway, and decide to pass a truck. You pull out to pass and notice a car approaching from the opposite direction. In about two seconds you gauge your speed, the speed of the oncoming car, the speed of the truck, and the distance you need in order to pass safely. With these calculations completed you decide whether or not to pass. Note, you have solved a complex problem in physics with enough accuracy to be correct most of the time (and be around to read this footnote). This is but another example of how quickly complex situations can be assessed in a manner much like Raiffa describes.

even under orders, if you were the only GI likely to do so? The answer to those questions for most people is "NO." Turner and Killian would argue that your refusal to initiate deviant action is largely a result of unconscious conformity to emergent group norms. Decision Theory suggests that emergent norms are not the only or even necessarily the most important factor. Rather, in each case acting alone would have *increased the costs of the activity*. Remember that each crowd member seeks to gain a minimax outcome, and the payoffs for various possible actions are *fundamentally dependent on the actions of others gathered at the scene*. If you decide to build the barricade and others join in, you're a "leader," maybe even a hero(ine). If you start to build the barricade and others desert you, you are a "schmuck." Arrest and/or suspension will likely follow, along with the ridicule implied by the existence of a norm which demeaned barricade building.

When Decision Theory is placed in the context of a group where the best outcome for a given individual fundamentally depends on what others will do, social scientists call the situation a "game." The term "game" is applied because in many ways, crowds resemble situations like poker, chess, and Monopoly. Each person wants to "win" and must consider what others are likely to do. In poker, for instance, before one bluffs one must judge the likelihood that the bluff will work.

Gaming in crowds is far more complicated than in usual recreational games. Let's take the Sheridan Road barricade as an example. As the students walked up the road, each had a variety of assessments of the situation and hopes for what might occur. Some wanted to go back to the dormitory, others wanted to do something more militant. When a student started to drag the fence across the road, a crowd gathered,

and an *opportunity* was generated. Many students did not know what to make of the situation, others had some tentative interpretation and activities they wished to see accomplished. As the gathering grew, students talked among themselves. Some of the conversations reflected attempts to understand themselves. Some of the conversations reflected attempts to understand the events, others approximated *negotiations*. One student would suggest an action (e.g., "let's go back to the dormitory") and another would counter with another proposal (e.g., "No, let's stay around and help these guys block Sheridan Road.") These interactions were not only quests for information, but attempts to *generate support for specific ideas*. Crowd members realized that any activity which would provide substantial rewards would have to be widely supported. Hence, participants were involved in a "game" in which they sought to advance their own interests by recruiting others. If no support for an idea was forthcoming, that idea was unlikely to provide high rewards.

What happens if a crowd member advocates an action which is not well received? He/she can continue to try to generate support for the idea, support someone else's proposal or suggest a compromise action, one less personally desirable, but which others are more likely to favor. Hence, one can view crowds as a kind of informal legislature. Participants try to gather support for their "program." These proposals typically reflect a compromise between what each individual desires and what is likely to be widely supported.[11]

Negotiation and the related attempts to understand the situation require exten-

---

11. Not everyone is busily advocating his position. Recall Shibutani's discussion of the variety of roles in rumor formation. That diversity is most applicable here.

sive communication. Verbal conversation, speeches, and loud pronouncements are obviously important. In addition, much of the communication involves symbols. In the cheating example, when one student broke his pencil in two and another threw a ball of paper against a window, they were indicating disgust and anger. Those actions were just as effective as a verbal statement like "I'm really teed off." In contrast, had a student reached down and taken off his shoes, that action would have carried little meaning (in that context). In short, ideas can be exchanged (a) verbally, (b) through objects like flags which function as symbols, and (c) through symbolic actions, which also carry important messages.

It should be clear that gaming approaches to collective behavior focus on the ways crowd members respond to their physical surrounding and the ways in which they try to gain individual rewards contingent on the actions of others. Space does not allow us to go into extensive detail, but one specific application will illustrate the potential of gaming perspectives.

One could postulate that before a crowd member decides to undertake an action such as looting a store, two basic issues are considered. First, the crowd member judges whether others will support the action. If the actor were to throw a brick through a store window and enter the store, would others join in? Second, what would be the payoffs if others did not join? Also, What would be the payoffs if they did? Assuming looting is the desired activity, the risks are likely to be reduced if others cooperate (by joining the action, or at least by not calling the police). One might formalize this process through the following equation:

$$P_{(ACT)} = f \left[(O_A - O_{\overline{A}}) \ P_{(SUP)} \right] \text{ FOR } O_A - O_{\overline{A}} \geqq O$$

$P_{(ACT)}$ is the probability that a person will begin the action, in this case, looting. O_A is the anticipated payoff (i.e., outcome) for acting $O_{\overline{A}}$ is the anticipated payoff for not acting. $P_{(SUP)}$ is the probability (i.e., certainty) of group support. The equation says that the probability that a person will initiate action is a function of the product of *net* anticipated payoffs (the rewards for acting minus the rewards for not acting) and the certainty of support.

Let's examine what the equation communicates. First the greater the anticipated rewards for acting compared to those for not acting, the more likely it is that a person will initiate action. Second, the more a crowd member thinks others will support the action, the more likely it is that action will be undertaken. Third, if the anticipated net rewards are zero (rewards for acting are no larger than for not acting) a person will not begin to act, even if support seems probable. Fourth, if the perceived likelihood of support is zero (the crowd member figures others will not cooperate) a person will not begin to act even if the activity could produce massive rewards with crowd support. In other words, a potential looter might really want to vandalize a store. But if support from others is not anticipated, the looting will not be undertaken. Fifth, a crowd member whose anticipated rewards are very large will begin to act even if the chances of support seem small. He/she will be more willing to "gamble" on the likelihood that others will join in. Sixth, a crowd member who thinks others are very likely to support an action will initiate action even if the anticipated rewards are very small. In other words, group support reduces the potential risks so significantly that he/she might as well loot. Seventh, all of these predictions are quantifiable so that specific alterations in anticipated payoffs and perceived support are immediately expressed in the likelihood that a person will initiate action. Indeed, that most interesting potential for the equation lies in its quantitative specificity which translates descriptive insights into testable propositions.

How plausible are foundations of the equation? Put yourself in the shoes of a student in Professor Smith's class. Let's suppose you figure there is no way you are going to pass the exam. Further, you have no objection to cheating under the circumstances, since Smith has treated the class unfairly. In short, you can anticipate substantially more rewards for cheating than for not cheating. However, you also have to consider whether people in the class will report you. If you really want to cheat, you will be more prepared to gamble that no one will "fink." For example, you probably would not go to the trouble of directly asking each person in the class whether he or she would report you. Rather, you would be satisfied with the events as they occurred, that is, that no one voiced strong disagreement after the final proposal was made. In contrast, if you figured you could probably get a legitimate "C" on the exam, you might be less willing to gamble that no one would turn you in. You'd want to determine if group solidarity was a sure thing. Since you could pass the exam without cheating, you would undertake the risk of cheating only if the risk was minimal. You would have potentially far more to lose by cheating if you could pass the exam than if you could not pass it.

Real crowds typically present far more complex game situations than our cheating example. Greater numbers of people are usually involved, the available information is more ambiguous, communication more

difficult, and the environment is more complicated and unstable. As a way of illustrating the approach that gaming perspectives advocate in analyzing actual crowds, we will briefly examine some important factors affecting crowd members who are trying to gauge the *probability of support* for a given action.

1. *The Number of People Acting in Ways which Support the Desired Actions of the Given Individual.* The effect of this variable may be "S" shaped (A Logistic Function) such that it alters the probability of support mostly through changes in its middle ranges (a tipping effect). If only a few people are acting, the effect on perceived support may be minimal. When most are acting the probability of support is already high (depending on other factors listed below). In other words, a specific functional form is postulated.[12]

2. *The Visibility of the Acting People.* If a crowd member is not aware that others are engaged in supportive actions, obviously variable #1 (the number of people acting) can have no impact on the probability of support. This variable suggests an important role for the environment in which the crowd is located and its physical arrangement in space.

First, a crowd's shape affects the visibility of crowd member activity. For example, a crowd

12. A graphic representation of this relationship might look like this:

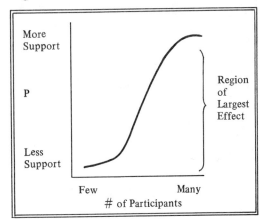

which weaves through several city blocks will prevent many crowd members from seeing any action around a corner. Each crowd member's view will depend on his/her location in relation to acting people. Consequently, not only will some crowds have structures which affect overall (aggregate) visibility, but crowd members may have differing abilities to see.

Second, crowd density will affect visibility. Its impact may be bell shaped: dense crowds and sparse crowds will substantially undercut the effect of crowd activity on perceived support. In high density crowds, it will be difficult to see more than a few neighboring individuals. Sparse crowds provide an unobstructed view, but much of the support inherent in group action is lost. Certain important advantages of concerted action are negated as density decreases because one is virtually acting alone. Note that again a functional form is suggested. Third, actions near the center of the crowd will be more easily seen by more people than actions on the fringes because the average (per person) distance from the events will be shorter. In addition, if the existence of supportive actions is spread by word of mouth, the information will spread more rapidly because the lines of communication will be on the average shorter.

Fourth, the amount of light will obviously affect what can be seen. Visibility will be greater during the day than at night unless artificial light is present. This might seem a trivial point were artificial light not a manipulable factor and, hence, relevant for social control. Indeed, the common use of bright search lights (at night) to intimidate crowds may actually facilitate mobilization.

Fifth, parts of a crowd may be at lower (or higher) elevation. Persons acting at points of high elevation will be more easily seen than those acting at lower elevations. The implications for aspiring leaders are clear.

3. *Ease of Interpreting the Actions of Others as Supportive.* Not only must people be seen acting, but their behavior must be understood as supporting the desired activities of the given crowd member (i.e., reducing the costs). There are several conditions which should aid each individual in deciding that the actions of others

are supportive. In general, these factors simplify the interpretative task.

First, if the behavior has symbolic components that communicate its meaning, ease of interpretations will be enhanced. Throwing a bag of urine at a policeman, for example, may carry a much clearer message than shoving some unidentified onlooker.

Second, behavior previously explained will be more easily interpreted than novel, undefined behavior. Thus, once the actions of Civil Disorder participants had been widely publicized, throwing a brick through a ghetto merchant's window could take on a protest meaning that might not have existed previously (Fogelson, 1971).[13]

Third, the more homogeneous the actions the easier the interpretation. There is simply less complexity to assimilate.

Fourth, the behavior of known people will be more easily interpreted than the actions of strangers. If a person is familiar, there will be more information with which to impute meaning.

Fifth, behavior which is similar to what a given individual desires will be more easily interpreted. The crowd member can more easily put himself in the other's shoes and understand actions, motives, and intent.

Sixth, behavior that is explained to crowd members will be more easily interpreted. In addition, if the explanation is consistent with norms (emergent or otherwise), it will be more readily understood. Here the role of "leaders" may be important since they can sometimes gain the attention of crowd members and interpret behavior.

4. *The Proximity of Acting People.* People acting near a given crowd member will be more likely to increase the probability of support for several reasons. First, they will be more visible. Second, potential strength in numbers differs if allies are proximate or at some distance. Crowd members will sense more support from actions nearby because charging "alone" into a police line, for example, with "support" from others a block away will closely approximate

13. Robert Fogelson, *Violence as Protest*, Doubleday, New York, 1971.

action with no support. Third, if a crowd is fairly dense, the only people visible to each individual will be those close by. Hence, if neighbors begin to act and if these are the only people visible, a crowd member might mistakenly think that the entire crowd was involved. His "sample" might indicate unanimity missing in the crowd as a whole.

To summarize, a gaming approach to crowds tries to explain why certain group actions appear. Collective behavior is viewed as a consequence of *Collective Decision-Making* involving compromises among participants. Each crowd member tries to make the most of the situation while constrained by the need for support from others. One inner city black cannot drive away 100 policeman, one prisoner cannot "liberate" a prison, and one tenant farmer cannot lynch an alleged rapist. For each to attain their goal, cooperation must be forthcoming. The same issues appear when police, soldiers, and even congressmen engage in collective behavior. A single policeman breaking ranks (against orders) and beating a demonstrator might well be dismissed and/or prosecuted for assault. (Though a simple reprimand is the usual result.) In contrast, if the entire police line breaks ranks, there is less chance of punishment.

Gaming approaches emphasize both details in the interactions between participants and environmental factors which shape behavior. As one might follow the history of a bill as it passes through a legislature, gaming provides tools with which to follow the life of a proposal for crowd action. Note that there is no *necessary* contradiction between gaming approaches and emergent norm views. The former may be seen as an extension of the latter. Concerted action in crowds may develop as a consequence of both unconscious con-

formity and Collective Decision-Making through gaming.[15]

Gaming approaches may be usefully applied to all sorts of crowds. However, the term Collective Decision-Making is usually reserved for crowds in which cooperation is necessary. One can specify three types.

First, crowds may be like those we have emphasized in which people are seeking to *do* something requiring support. One can think of these as *active* crowds. In active crowds people attempt to directly affect a situation themselves.

Second, in some crowds people are seeking to *communicate* to someone who can affect their situation. For example, if the students in Smith's class had decided to march *en mass* to the University President's office chanting "We all know, Smith must go", the action would be characterized as communicative. Since they cannot themselves fire Smith, they are trying to express their grievances to someone who can. Of course, our example was an instance of direct action, not communication.

Third, in some crowds people seek neither to alter a situation themselves, nor to

14. Richard A. Berk, "A Gaming Approach to Crowd Behavior" American Journal of Sociology, June, 1974.
15. In order to be fair, a critique of gaming approaches should be presented. All other views have been assessed in terms of strengths and weaknesses. In an important sense, that critique exists throughout earlier sections of this volume. All of the approaches that emphasize irrational behavior in crowds, (suggestability, contagion, and so on) represent positions which oppose gaming perspectives. However, there are other issues one might raise. First, since gaming implies action based on unobserved pyschological states, it could be difficult to test. How might one know whether a person is really trying to maximize gains? Second, there is a fundamental question whether people really consider the factors that gaming approaches require. Perhaps behavior is a result of factors having little to do with considerations of costs and benefits?

convince some person or organization to alter the situation. Instead they wish to simply express themselves. They do not intend for someone to hear them; *expression is an end in itself.* For example, in many fundamentalist church services much of the activity involves chanting, singing, and clapping. Though some of these expressions are directed at God, much of the activity is primarily for the benefit of the participants. It's fun to clap and sing in a group, and the enjoyment derived is an end in itself. Note, the activity is cooperative since one person cannot be a chorus. Further, if the services are loosely organized, people have to decide when they will engage in the group activity of singing or clapping. It is much like building the barricade. To start singing alone when no one else is ready to join would be at least embarrassing. Each participant must pick up cues in order to gauge what kind of group activity will gain support and when that support might be fourth coming. Hence, the justification for calling the expression *cooperative.*

It should be emphasized that in most crowds people are likely to be engaged in direct action, communicating to those who can affect the situation and expressing themselves as an end in itself, all at the same time. Nevertheless, when crowds exist in which one of these forms is most salient, it can be useful to employ one of the three categories. However, utmost care should be taken when such labels are used. Recall that central tendencies should not be confused with homogeniety.

But what about panics? Gaming approaches explain panics in terms of *competition,* not cooperation. Put yourself in the proverbial crowded theater when a fire starts. It is obvious to the entire audience that a rapid exit is the best way to avoid be-ing burned. It may also be apparent that the safest way to get out would be for everyone to move quickly towards the exits in an orderly fashion. Now, let's suppose someone starts running to the exit. One inference is that the person is behaving emotionally and not acting in his/her best interests. However, this person may know something you don't. Maybe there is insufficient time for everyone to escape unharmed. If so, those who get out first may be the only ones to survive. In that case, each person's best strategy is to run like hell for exits. What would you do if you saw several people acting this way? Would you gamble that the "panicky" members of the audience are really wrong in their assessments; that there really is time for all to escape? Or would you join the "stampede." These kinds of crowds are called competitive because "scarce resources" (in this case too few exits) dictate that each person's interests are best served by competing with others. Participants are not seeking cooperation, for if the resources really are scarce, the best strategy is "each man for himself." In cooperative crowds, people can maximize their payoffs by working with others. In competitive crowds, people try to maximize their rewards by struggling against each other. Notice that both Decision Theory and gaming are appropriate; however, the nature of the game has changed

There are many other ways to classify crowds than the typologies just described. For example, when focusing just on cooperative crowds it is sometimes useful to characterize the degree to which salient motives (as central tendencies) are concrete or abstract. In American Civil Disorders, a black rioter might have looted a store because its owner had been selling inferior merchandise. The target involved one specific shop keeper. Or a store might have been looted though the merchant's actions were not really the issue. Whites as a group were being attacked. Finally, a store might have been looted because it represented American society and an unfair distribution of consumer goods. Neither the individual merchant, nor his ethnic group was the real target. The rioter had abstracted his/her grievances until the basic social order was indicted. Put more formally, the target might involve a given individual or condition, a group of individuals or class of conditions, or the society itself. In our example, these three levels of abstraction are the individual merchant, white people, and American society.

The level of abstraction in the rioter's motives can have important implications for the maintenance of social order. In general, the more abstract the motive, the greater the threat to the society. Black rioters whose primary intent was to "rip off" color TV's were not nearly as dangerous as rioters wishing to drive all whites from the inner city. Most dangerous were rioters seeking to challenge capitalism. They hoped to change the basic nature of society and were less easily diverted and diffused. However, it is important to keep in mind that motive is of little import if it cannot be effectively implemented. In American Civil Disorders, motives rarely involved attacks on capitalism, and revolutionaries were unable to gain much support. The disturbances were far closer to classic Bread Riots in which people sought to remedy specific grievances. In American Civil Disorders, some people looted for profit, some people vandalized shops judged exploitative, some attacked white owned stores as surrogates for whites

in general, some participated primarily to call attention to grievances ignored by white society, but few hoped to alter the basic social order. Hence, American Civil Disorders were largely *active* and *communicative* with moderately abstract motives which ultimately posed little threat to American Society. The actions were aimed at reslicing the American pie of consumer goods and services rather than baking the pie anew.

SUMMARY AND CONCLUSIONS

The material presented in this chapter could be productively integrated. No single approach tells the complete story, but as a body of knowledge provides a useful foundation for future work. We have come a long way from herd-like descriptions of crowd activity, and if there is one overall conclusion, it is that collective behavior is not some unique type of human interaction. Collective behavior occurs every day in a variety of situations. We are constantly being bombarded by informal group pressures and many of our contacts with others approximate cooperative and/or competitive games. Hence, human rationality is no less operative in crowds than in any other circumstance. We all operate with blinders, and though they may differ from situation to situation, they obscure the world nonetheless.

For Further Reading

Much of the material discussed in this chapter is so recent that it can be found only in rather technical discussions in professional journals. The most readable exception exists in Roger Brown's textbook, *Social Psychology* (New York: Free Press, 1965, Chapter 14). Another possibility is my article in the Short and Wolfgang reader cited earlier, "The Emergence of Muted Violence in Crowd Behavior: A Case Study of an Almost Race Riot." If neither of these suffice, the best bet would be to look over sources cited in the text of this chapter.

Glossary

The glossary must be used with care. The definitions provided are at best shorthand for some rather complex notions. Further, different theorists discussed in the book often use the same words in somewhat different ways. The glossary is no substitute for reading the text.

Alienation—A psychological state characterized by a feeling of rootlessness and confusion about societal norms.

Anarchism—A political philosophy characterized by a belief that the State is evil: in practice, advocacy of the destruction of all large societal institutions. Often an alternative form of society is envisioned in which people organize themselves into smaller groups that are run by the people they serve.

Assimilation—The tendency of rumors to become more coherent and consistent with preexisting views of people communicating the rumor.

Circular Reaction—A theoretical process proposed by Herbert Blumer in which crowd members react to each other without critically examining their situation or the communications of other crowd members.

Civil Disorder—Collective behavior usually resulting in personal injury and property damage in which the targets of crowd members are typically private property and representatives of societal institutions. Though the crowd members and social control agents (e.g., police) may be of different races or ethnic groups, there are rarely physical confrontations between groups of citizens of different races or ethnic groups.

Collective Behavior—Relatively spontaneous, transitory, and concerted behavior by people in face-to-face contact where considerable interpersonal cooperation and/or competition is necessary for the group activity to occur (See Chapter I).

Collective Decision-Making—The process by which individuals in crowds arrive at concerted action though communication, negotiation, and compromise.

Contagion—A metaphorical "explanation" of the causes of collective behavior in which crowd members get caught up in the emotions of the moment and lose their self-control and ability to reason. Crowd members "catch" this mood from each other.

Contagion Theory—An outdated group of theories of collective behavior in which "contagion" is used to explain the crowd activity.

Convergence Theory—An outdated group of theories of collective behavior in which crowds are explained as a product of concerted activity by people who bring similar motives to the scene.

Craze—Collective behavior characterized by a generalized belief primarily involving wish fulfillment.

Decision Theory—A prescriptive systematic scheme to assist in the making of decisions under conditions of uncertainty.

Due Process—Mechanisms of a legal system which are designed to protect citizens *arbitrary* curtailment of their rights. For example, American citizens are not supposed to serve time in prison without a "trial."

Emergent Norms—Norms which develop at the scene of collective behavior and which guide and shape the activities of crowd members.

Epistemology—The science or theory of *the method* of knowing about things. It addresses the question, "how do you know what you know?" (see footnote 1 chapter II)

Frustration-Aggression Hypothesis—A psychological theory which claims that frustrated people are likely to be aggressive.

Game Theory—A mathematical formulation which indicates under certain specific conditions the "best" strategy a person should follow when his/her rewards depend on the actions of others.

Generalized Belief—A concept developed by Neil Smelser to characterize the mental processes of collective behavior participants. Generalized beliefs are a necessary condition for collective behavior according to Smelser. They are commonly held and are naive, magical views of the situation.

Group Mind—A concept developed by LeBon to describe the homogeneity of thought and behavior he believed to exist in crowds. The crowd was an entity unto itself, analogous to a biological organism, which had a life of its own over and above the individuals who participated.

Herd Instinct—An outdated view that there exists an instinct common to all people which makes them vulnerable to "contagion" in crowds.

Hostile Outburst—Collective behavior characterized by a generalized belief which specifies a specific target for aggressive action.

Identification—A psychological process by which a person subconsciously fantasizes to be someone else.

Ideology—Broad ideas and beliefs about the nature of society often held in common by members of a given social class, political group, racial or ethnic group, or nation.

Introjection—A psychological process by which a person subconsciously incorporates someone else's values as his/her own.

J-Curve—A line on a graph representing a period of raising quality of life followed by a period of sharp decline.

Kerner Commission—An investigatory body authorized by President Johnson to examine the causes of Civil Disorders of the late 1960's and make recommendations to prevent such outbreaks in the future.

Leveling—The process by which it is alleged that heterogeneous individuals are transformed into a crowd where people think and behave alike.

Mass Society—A societal condition in which citizens do not feel attached to societal institutions and in which societal elites are especially vulnerable to political pressure from the citizens.

Methodology—The techniques and processes employed to undertake empirical research. For example, a survey is a kind of methodology.

Milling—A process prior to the beginning of crowd behavior when crowd members move about talking to one another.

Mobilization—A process by which a group of individuals are drawn into collective behavior through a generalized belief.

Necessary Conditions—"Causes" of a given phenomenon which must be present for that phenomenon to occur. However, if these "causes" are present it does not mean that the phenomenon will have to occur; it only may occur. For example, one must have two antagonistic racial groups for a race riot to occur. But, the existence of two antagonistic racial groups does not mean that a race riot will inevitably take place.

Omnipotence—A condition in infancy where the infant is unable to distinguish his/her body from the environment and hence feels at one with the environment.

Operationalization—The process by which theoretical concepts are transformed into measurable entities. For example one might operationalize a person's education by the years of formal schooling completed.

Panic—Collective behavior characterized by a generalized belief emphasizing flight from the scene.

Precipitating Incident—Events which "trigger" collective behavior.

Psychological Determinism—The theory that no human behavior is accidental, rather that all human behavior has motives.

Race Riot—Collective behavior usually resulting in destruction of property and personal injury where members of one race or ethnic group attack members of another race or ethnic group.

Rationality—The thought processes described by Decision Theory in which costs and benefits are weighed before action is undertaken.

Revolution of Rising Expectations—A period of unrest caused by the aspirations of people outstripping the ability of a society to meet those aspirations.

Riff-Raff Theory—An inaccurate theory that American Civil Disorders of the 1960's were caused by criminals, "outside agitators," and people from the lowest socioeconomic levels of the inner city.

Rumor—Information gathered informally which is used to define and interpret an ambiguous situation.

Sharpening—The tendency of rumor to emphasize some details at the expense of others.

Social Strain—A poor fit (often conflict) between the goals or ideals of a society and the performance of the society. It can also mean the perception by citizens of the poor fit, or conflict between the goals themselves.

Structural Conduciveness—The existence of societal conditions which are necessary (but not sufficient) for collective behavior.

Subconscious Motives—Motives of which an individual is unaware and which an individual cannot easily bring to awareness.

Sufficient Conditions—"Causes" of a given phenomenon which if present are always followed by the phenomenon. For example, in the physical sciences sending an electrical charge into a stick of dynamite is a sufficient condition for an explosion.

Suggestability—A psychological state in which crowd members are easily influenced by each other and by crowd leaders. Crowd members lose their ability to reason as individuals and get "swept up" in the crowd activity.

Taxations Populaire—Riots by French citizens before the industrial revolution (i.e., before the middle of the nineteenth century) in which citizens faced with inflationary prices for grain and bread seized these commodities at what they felt to be "just" prices.

Unit of Analysis—The level of aggregation to be employed in a particular theory or empirical study. For example, individuals can be a unit of analysis, or a crowd can be a unit of analysis, or a social class can be a unit of analysis.

Value Added—A manufacturing process by which raw materials take on additional economic value as they are transformed into a finished product. Smelser borrowed the term to describe steps leading to collective behavior.

Walker Report—One of a series of reports issued by Lyndon Johnson's National Commission on the Causes and Prevention of Violence. The report generated considerable controversy when it blamed much of the violence surrounding the 1968 Democratic convention in Chicago on the "overreaction" of Chicago police.

Wish Fulfillment—The theory that all human motives reflect the seeking of desirable outcomes.

Index

absolute deprivation, 47-48
active crowds, 73
Agnew, Spiro, 12
alienation, 37-39, 46
ambivalence, 30
assimilation, 62

Blumer, Herbert, 31-33, 43
bread riots, 12, 33, 75. See also Taxations
    Populaire

Carmichael, Stokely, 12
chartism, 12
circular reaction, 32-33, 34, 61
civil disorders, 10-11, 12, 17, 25, 39, 43,
    44, 50, 61, 74-75
collective behavior
    characteristics of, 3-4, 5, 7-8, 57-59
    examples of, 2-7, 54-56
    data quality, 13-19
collective decision-making, 54, 58, 62,
    64-67, 69-70, 73. See also gaming
    theory, rumor, decision theory
collective excitement, 3, 63
communicative crowds, 73
conformity. See also homogeneity,
    Emergent Norms
contagion, 16, 20, 23-26, 32, 33-34, 65
convergence theory, 34-35
craze, 8, 41

Davies, James C., 49, 50
decision theory, 59-61, 63, 67, 68, 74
    See also gaming theory
dependence, 29, 30
Dollard, John, 47
draft riots, 12-13

emergence, 23. See also Emergent Norms
Emergent Norms, 64-67, 68. See also
    collective decision-making
expressive crowds, 41, 43, 44, 73-74

Feirabend, Ivo R., 50
Feirabend, Rosalind L., 50
fickleness, 24, 30
Fogelson, Robert, 72
Freud, Sigmund, 20, 26-31, 32
frustration-aggression hypotheses, 46-53

gaming theory, 67-75. See also decision
    theory, rationality
generalized belief, 42-43, 44, 45-56, 57
group mind, 16
Gurr, Ted R., 49, 50, 51

herd instinct, 16, 20
homogeneity, 8, 18-19, 31, 33, 34, 35, 45,
    57, 62-63, 64-67, 69. See also
    mental unity, generalized belief,
    contagion, suggestability, circular
    reaction, hypnotism, convergence
    theory, rumor, Emergent Norms,
    collective decision-making
hostile outburst, 41-42, 43, 44
hypnotism, 20, 22, 23, 25, 32, 34

identification, 29, 31, 32, 34
ideology, 11-13
imitation, 23, 24, 25
introjection, 30

j-curve, 49-50
Johnson, Lyndon B., 10, 50

Kerner Commission, 10
Killian, Lewis M., 64-67
Kornhauser, William, 36-40, 45, 46

leaders, 22-26, 29-31, 34, 43, 58
LeBon, Gustav, 20-26, 27, 28, 30, 31, 32,
    34, 36, 37, 40, 43